# Praise for
# The Brave New World of Healthcare

"Resilience and fortitude are required to preach hard choices to a profligate nation. But Governor Richard Lamm has been the dean of the school of hard choices for at least two decades. Here he holds a stark mirror up to an American society willing to steal from its children and bankrupt the next generation. In scalding language fueled by scorn for an age where accountability and responsibility are sacrificed to greed and comfort, Governor Lamm uses the health care finance debacle as a metaphor for a nation unwilling to pay its own way. Though he risks being marginalized and dismissed as some early twenty-first-century prophet Jeremiah crying shame on an irresponsible society, he will surely be honored by our children for his courage and his integrity on their behalf."

*Gary Hart*
*Former United States Senator*

"Sooner or later—and let us hope sooner—we Americans are going to have to ask some tough questions about a health care system that can't insure our working families and health costs that are rising at six times the rate of inflation. Dick Lamm asks those tough questions—and comes up with some answers. You may or may not agree with them, but unless our political leaders confront them as he has, we'll never be able to guarantee all Americans decent health care at a reasonable cost."

*Michael Dukakis*
*Former Governor of Massachusetts*
*and Democratic Presidential Candidate*

"Richard Lamm has never been a "throw money at it" politician, and yet he never hesitates to tackle injustices with his keen mind and wisdom. What greater injustice for Americans can there be than having 44 million of our fellow citizens having no health insurance? This book should be mandatory reading for every citizen. There is no one better than Lamm to challenge our thinking about how to rectify this wrong."

*Patricia Schroeder*
*President and CEO of the Association of American Publishers*
*and Former Congresswoman*

# Brave
# New World
# of Healthcare
# REVISITED

# Brave
# New World
# of Healthcare
# REVISITED

## What Every American Needs to Know
## about Our Healthcare Crisis

## Richard D. Lamm
## and Andy Sharma

FULCRUM
GOLDEN, COLORADO

Library of Congress Cataloging-in-Publication Data
2012034569

Printed in the United States of America
0 9 8 7 6 5 4 3 2 1

Design by Jack Lenzo

Fulcrum Publishing
4690 Table Mountain Dr., Ste. 100
Golden, CO 80403
800-992-2908 • 303-277-1623
www.fulcrumbooks.com

# Contents

Acknowledgments...........................................................................ix

Preface.......................................................................................xi

**ONE:** Aging ...............................................................................1

**TWO:** "The Problem": Thinking about the US Healthcare System .......31

**THREE:** Rebuilding the House of Healthcare ...................................99

**FOUR:** Rethinking the Institutions of an Aging Society....................137

**CONCLUSION** .........................................................................153

Epilogue: Final Thoughts by Governor Lamm......................................159

Notes .......................................................................................167

Selected Bibliography .................................................................171

Permissions ..............................................................................173

About the Authors ......................................................................175

# Acknowledgments

No TREES GROW TO THE SKY, AND NO ELEMENT OF THE US NATIONAL BUDGET CAN grow at more than twice the rate of inflation. Yet that is the rate of growth of healthcare during my professional lifetime. A series of healthcare decisions lie in our immediate future that will make our moral compasses gyrate, yet we have not even begun talking about them. Their difficulty will be compounded as we retire the baby boomers and find that Social Security financing and long-term care needs are competing for these same dollars.

This is not "just another issue." I believe this is a nation-threatening issue. The numbers required to finance the future are gargantuan and began to come due when the first wave of baby boomers start to retire in 2011. They threaten to undercut the economy, crowd out other important public needs, and increase generational tensions. Instead of moving to meet this challenge, our nation gives tax cuts instead—with borrowed money! This raises what is to me a fascinating issue: are our institutions as we have developed them equal to the magnitude of our problems? Can our democracy make hard choices?

For most of American history, politicians were able to give voters more and more. We have a rich continent, populated by a creative and hardworking people. We have overcome a number of obstacles. But we have also become an overindulged people who seem to have lost the ability to tighten our belts and make sacrifices for our children and our future.

Healthcare presents not only challenging funding problems but also fascinating ethical and policy issues. Simply put, we have invented more healthcare than we can afford to deliver to everyone. This book represents my odyssey into healthcare ever since the midseventies, when I realized how much it was driving my budget.

I have been greatly enriched in my thinking about health-care by Victor Fuchs, Haavi Morreim, David Eddy, and Robert Blank, among others. I am in their debt for ways that I cannot fully acknowledge.

I would like to acknowledge my lovely wife, Dottie, who has accompanied me to countless hospitals and clinics around the globe, many in the third world, with only the occasional interesting dinner with a dedicated doctor for her reward.

—Dick Lamm

I BELIEVE WELL-REASONED PUBLIC POLICY REQUIRES GOOD INFORMATION. IN OTHER words, policy makers need to have a thorough and up-to-date understanding of key issues. My hope is that this book serves such a function for healthcare.

I would like to acknowledge my former professors at DePaul, Loyola, and the University of North Carolina at Chapel Hill. I have learned much from them and am pleased I could impart some of my knowledge to the readers of this book. I would also like to thank my father, my mother, who passed away from breast cancer in 2009, my older brother, my sister-in-law, and my niece and nephew for their support. Lastly, I want to thank Amanda E. Melvin for reading several versions of rough drafts.

—Andy Sharma

# Preface

MY WIFE, DOTTIE, SURVIVED BREAST CANCER. I AM FOREVER GRATEFUL TO THE SKILL AND caring of an excellent group of doctors and a good hospital. There is no doubt in my mind that we owe her health and her life to the brilliance of the US healthcare system. Cancer had spread to her lymph nodes, and the statistics were very much against her. Now, nearly thirty years later, I awake every morning next to a living testament to the genius and effectiveness of American medicine.

But I also have children. And increasingly, I see the healthcare system consuming massive resources that are desperately needed in other parts of the economy if we are to leave our children a sustainable society. When I graduated from college, in 1960, America spent 6 percent of our gross national product (GNP) on education, 6 percent on defense, and 6 percent on healthcare. In 2011, we spent 6 percent on education, approximately 5 percent on defense, and 17 percent on healthcare. That's approximately $2.5 trillion a year on healthcare; before long, we shall spend $3 trillion a year. We spend 50 percent more than any of our economic competitors, and this expenditure has been rising at twice the rate of inflation during my professional lifetime—unsustainable in the new world marketplace. Yet, for all of our spending, we do not exceed our competitors in any basic health statistic, except life expectancy, at the age of 80. Granted, we have marvelous doctors and hospitals that often achieve the miraculous, but from a public policy standpoint, where every dollar is important, it is difficult to see what justifies such an extraordinary level of expenditure.

Compare categories of US spending as a percentage of our GNP:

| Year | Education | Defense | Healthcare |
|------|-----------|---------|------------|
| 1960 | 6% | 6% | 6% |
| 2011 | 6% | 5% | 17% |

Do we get our money's worth? Reflecting the opinion of most experts who study healthcare systems, international expert George Schieber observes:

> In comparison with other major industrial countries, health care in the United States costs more per person and per unit of service, is less accessible to a larger portion of its citizens, is provided at a more intensive level and offers comparatively poor gross outcomes.

American expectations for healthcare over the last thirty years have been developed during the most massive transfer of wealth into one sector (healthcare) that history has ever seen. Healthcare is a fiscal black hole into which we can pour all of our children's future. Yet we are no healthier than many nations that spend far less, and we leave 50.7 million Americans uncovered by health insurance. Americans now spend on average approximately $8,000 per person on healthcare. Because we spend more doesn't mean we get more, nor does it mean we are spending this amount wisely. Economists worry that we are unbalancing our economy and that it's not wise national policy to spend one dollar out of every six dollars of our gross domestic product (GDP) on healthcare. Social policy experts point out myriad other public needs that are underfunded, yet polls show that Americans regard healthcare as one of the most important priorities; most Americans want to spend more, not less, on healthcare. That is politically important because in a democracy we generally get what we want, but is it wise public policy? Do we really know what we are doing?

The pressures will only increase. We live in the age of bionic body parts, a growing number of which are in common use. Some experts predict that, in this century, there will be human beings with more than 50 percent of their body weight in bionic parts.

There is hardly a part of the human body that medical science is not reworking, either as a transplant or in the way of repair or revitalization. Motors smaller than a hair are now available to move through our circulatory system and complete microscopic cell repair. We have mapped the human genome and soon will be able to give people a biomap telling them with a large degree of predictability what diseases they will develop and at what ages. Yesterday's science fiction stories are quietly becoming reality in today's medical journals, and most of these procedures are awesomely expensive. An aging society should keep in mind health economist Victor Fuchs's words: "The appetite for healthcare is infinitely expandable, since it is almost always possible to secure some marginal increased benefit by fulfilling wants or desires for more treatment."

If US healthcare were a separate nation, it would have one of the largest economies in the world. This unprecedented and unsustainable growth of expenditures has distorted our expectations from the healthcare system and masked the necessity to make some hard choices. We have developed the illusion of endless pools of money that will allow us to do everything medically for everybody without restraint. Most Americans have come to view healthcare as a right, and we want everything that might do us some good and want someone else to pay for it. Then we want these expectations enforced by lawsuits and even a Patient's Bill of Rights.

No item in any budget can grow forever at more than twice the normal rate of inflation, which healthcare has averaged over the last forty years. Princeton economist Uwe Reinhardt has estimated that at the rate of growth in healthcare spending for the last thirty years, by 2065 America will be spending 100 percent of its GDP on healthcare. He knows that this could never happen, but he uses it to illustrate that the status quo in healthcare is unsustainable. No trees grow to the sky. Something has to give. No nation can live by healthcare alone. But it isn't healthcare alone that America has to worry about. What compounds the problem and keeps policy makers up at night is that Social Security is also poised to make incredible and unsustainable demands on the public treasury. Many fiscal chickens are simultaneously coming home to roost. Major structural flaws have appeared in two of America's most popular social programs, healthcare and Social Security, yet we act as if they will repair themselves. Michael Kinsley, writing in *Time* magazine, captured America's denial of reality:

> The central problem of American politics [is] the inability of the electorate to deal with the hard reality we all had to learn as small children: that some of something usually means less of something else. . . . Our refusal to acknowledge that trade-offs are necessary . . . makes intelligent debate about . . . trade-offs impossible.

Americans can reasonably expect a lot, but not as much as we have come to feel entitled to. My aging body has the potential to keep my grandchildren from going to college. Healthcare can easily crowd out too many other important things we have to do with our limited funds. We need to start a national dialogue, and start it soon, on what we can reasonably expect of and realistically afford in our medical miracles. Americans want and expect what no nation can ever deliver: all the healthcare a technologically advanced society can develop and the resolution of our every health-related anxiety, while others help us pay for spare-no-cost medicine. Such a system is unsustainable, unaffordable, and inequitable and needs to be substantially amended and revised.

# ONE

# Aging

## The Demographic Trap

THE ANCIENT GREEKS BELIEVED THE GREATEST TRAGEDIES OCCUR WHEN WELL-MEANING, intelligent, caring humans invite disaster because they cannot see the big picture or understand new circumstances. A chorus warns them of impending disaster, but they do not hear. American public policy makers are ignoring a chorus of commissions and experts who are telling America that the baby boom is turning into the grandparent boom—with grave implications to America's future. We are consuming more than we produce, spending more than we earn, and borrowing money from our children to maintain lifestyles and government services.

## Demographics and Aging

ONE OF THE GREAT CHALLENGES IN AMERICA'S FUTURE IS TO RETIRE THE BABY BOOMERS without bankrupting the country or unduly burdening future generations. This demographic tidal wave is creeping up on America and could soon overwhelm American public policy. Yesterday's baby boom is tomorrow's grandparent boom. This demographic revolution presents us with some interrelated challenges, of which healthcare is the most troubling. How do we fund present programs for the elderly, let alone expand those programs for twice as many elderly? How do we adapt and fund our retirement and healthcare systems for an America of many more elderly citizens, fewer children, and exploding technologies? What are the social and political consequences of running a society whose average age will be approximately twice the average age as during our nation's first two hundred years? How do we add desperately needed long-term care to costs already out of control? If we act soon, we can answer these questions rationally, prepare for our future, and avoid steep economic decline. But if we wait, we will be forced to make draconian decisions.

America is getting older—fast. In 1900, we could expect to live 47.3 years; by 2010, we could expect to reach the age of 78. It is likely that those born early in this century can expect to live to 85. We are not only increasing the number and percentage of elderly, but the elderly themselves are getting older as modern medicine performs its miracles and a larger percentage of our population lives beyond 75. The fastest-growing demographic cohort in the United States is people over 100; the second-fastest-growing cohort is people over 85. (America has approximately 5.7 million people over the age of 85 and 75,000 over the age of 100.) America is expected to double the percentage of people over 85 between 1990 and 2030. It is estimated that we will have as many as 17.6 million Americans over the age of 85 by the middle of this century. The baby boomers at the end of their lives will continue to cause distortions to American demographics and challenges to American public policy.

These two aging trends had a great impact on the general demographic growth of the twentieth century. Since 1900, the population of the United States has tripled. The population of those over 65 has grown ten times, and the population of those over 85 has grown thirty times. This trend will continue. More than 10 percent of the elderly have at least one child who is over age 65. These realities will push us into uncharted territory for public policy.

Extended longevity is clearly good news for us individually. We are going to live longer and have more health and life than any generation in human history. A vast majority of babies born today will live past their 65<sup>th</sup> birthday, while fifty years ago less than 30 percent lived to see their 65<sup>th</sup> birthday.[1] Today's senior citizens have unprecedented and wonderful opportunities for a dignified and active retirement.

It is, however, a mixed blessing for American public policy, for some significant challenges come with this good news. Compounding the increase in life expectancy and the sheer number of elderly is a third demographic revolution taking place: the drop in the birthrate. People age from the moment they are born, but societies do not automatically age. Societies can get younger or older depending on how long people live and how many children are born to the average woman. The entire developed world is getting older. In 1957, a woman, on average, would bear 3.8 children. Today, she has 2.0. During the last half of the twentieth century, an extraordinarily large generation was followed by an extraordinarily small generation. It is this higher proportion of both elderly and "oldest-old" (over 85) that so compounds the challenges facing an aging society with a lower birthrate.

Soon America will be a vastly different society. Allan Pifer and Lydia Bronte observe:

> By the middle of the [twenty-first] century, when this revolution has run its course, the impacts will have been at least as powerful as that of any of the great economic and social movements of the past—movements such as the conquest and subsequent closing of the frontier, the successive waves of European immigration, the development of our great cities, or, from more recent times, the post–WWII baby boom, the civil rights and women's movements, the massive influx of women into the paid labor force, the revolution in sexual mores, and the decay of many of our large urban centers. All these developments have had a profound effect on our nation, but the aging of the population will certainly have an equal, if not greater impact.[2]

The United States is not alone in this demographic challenge. Worldwide, approximately 700 million people, 11 percent of the present population, are age 60 or older. The World Bank warns that "the world faces a looming old age crisis," and it estimates that by 2030, individuals over age 60 will number 1.5 billion, making up 16 percent of the world's population. The problem will be particularly acute for developed countries where pension funds are headed toward bankruptcy under this demographic avalanche.

"This is the first time humans have altered the age structure of the population," says University of Chicago demographer Jay Olshansky. Another scholar estimates that more than two-thirds of the improvement in longevity, from prehistoric times to the present, took place in the twentieth century.

The results of this demographic change are in some ways predictable, in others, unknowable. Without change in the current trends, America in 2050 will be a very different place, warn Jacob Siegel and Cynthia Tauber:

> Very high proportions of elderly persons and very high dependency ratios accompanied by continuing low fertility and very low mortality could have profound social and economic consequences. Education, healthcare, housing, recreation and work life would be affected by the changes in age structure described. There could be severe dislocations in the economy as it tries to adjust to the changing needs for jobs, goods and services. Tax rates could become oppressively high and serve as a disincentive to work. Younger workers will be called on for larger and larger financial contributions to the federal treasury on behalf of older nonworkers.[3]

The public policy dilemma is that we forged a majority of our most politically sacred social programs assuming a growing number of children and a shorter average longevity. The new demographic requires us to reform the programs built on the old demographic assumptions. It will not be easy.

There are essentially two ways a society can provide healthcare and retirement benefits for the elderly: (1) a society can prefund these programs like most of the private sector does, or (2) it can develop a social insurance scheme where one generation is obligated to take care of its parents in turn for their children's obligation to take care of them.

In the 1880s, Baron von Bismarck set up the first social insurance system in Germany and set the retirement age at 65—a number that most of the rest of the industrial world adopted. The catch is that life expectancy in Germany in the 1880s was 47. It is no trick to retire people at 65 when life expectancy is 47. Few retirees and many children make for an actuarially sound retirement program.

But one generation's solution is often another generation's problem. In 1967, Nobel Prize winner Paul Samuelson wrote in *Newsweek*: "The beauty about social insurance is that it is actuarially unsound. Everyone who reaches retirement age is given benefit privileges that far exceed anything he has paid." How can this be? He explained: "The national product is growing at compound interest rates and can be expected to do so as far ahead as the eye cannot see. . . . A growing nation is the greatest Ponzi game ever contrived."

Well-meaning, well-motivated, myopic people are putting America's future in jeopardy. Understanding that social insurance, which does have elements of a Ponzi scheme, has to be completely revised is one of the greatest challenges in America's future. The new reality is that neither equity nor social justice can be purchased today by passing on the cost to the next generation tomorrow. You cannot create social justice today on a layaway program charging tomorrow's taxpayers.

Would I have voted for Social Security in 1935 and for Medicare in 1965? Yes, of course, but the challenge of avoiding public policy tragedies is to understand when circumstances have changed.

The challenge of an aging society is to fund its compassion with its own money—not its children's. Social justice and intergenerational equity must consider both rich/poor justice and today/tomorrow justice. However unpopular, we must do this for our kids' sake.

Alas, a day of reckoning is upon us. Our national product is no longer growing at compound rates, our unfunded liabilities are exploding, and our social insurance scheme is running out of players. One of America's greatest challenges is to adapt to an aging society before the game is up.

## Are We Adding Years of Health or Years of Disability?

MODERN MEDICINE HAS EXTENDED BOTH LIVING AND DYING, AND IT IS IMPORTANT that public policy ask, are we adding more years of life worth living? Are we adding years of health or years of disability? Health expenditure per person declines from birth to early adulthood and then rises continuously into old age. The history of the last thirty years is that the elderly used more healthcare than those under age 65, and those over 85 years of age had the highest use and most expensive healthcare. We live longer, we are healthier at any particular age, and a smaller percentage of the elderly are in nursing homes, but the growth in numbers of elderly make an aging society more and more expensive.

Historically, lower mortality has led to increases of morbidity and disability. Some experts argue that there will develop a "compression of morbidity" in which we will live healthy older lives and then die fast. This contention is a long way from being proved but seems to be supported by recent evidence. We do know that the average health status for the elderly is generally improving and disabilities are declining while the numbers of elderly are increasing. Those 85 and older were only 7.5 percent of the total aged in 1970; they will soon be more than 14 percent of the elderly.[4] So at any given age, the elderly as a group are healthier, but more of them live on to develop disabilities. As J. M. Guralnik wisely observed:

> What is particularly ominous . . . is that (because most reduction in disability prior to death will occur in the younger-old population) most of the disability prior to death in the future will occur among those dying at age 85 and older, where the disability may in large part be what we might think of as difficult to prevent or "hard core." This would include diseases

such as Alzheimer's disease and degenerative arthritis, and perhaps more important, from the co-occurrence of multiple disability diseases.[5]

As one group of experts, led by James Lubitz, put it, "Our findings are suggestive of a steady or growing percentage of severely disabled people in a population whose overall average health status is improving." Individually, the average 75-year-old is healthier and has fewer chronic and disabling conditions, and disability in America is declining at an accelerated pace. The percentage of people over 65 with disabilities fell 1.6 percent per year from 1989 through 1994 and 2.6 percent a year from 1994 to 1999. But we still consume more healthcare the older we get. Our success in reducing disability is offset by increasing life expectancy.

Most of us do not want to die diapered and demented in a forgotten corner of a nursing home. The National Institute on Aging estimates we now have 4 million people with Alzheimer's disease. By 2050, it expects to see Alzheimer's disease in perhaps 15 million Americans. What will this mean for long-term care in the United States? What burden will we all impose on our children as we live on and on and on? The average American woman can already expect to spend more years caring for her parents than she spent caring for her children.

The average elderly person has 4.4 chronic conditions, some of which are minor, but many are very serious. As we get older, these degenerative diseases often interact with each other and have become the leading cause of death among the elderly in the developed world. Experts generally agree that we have postponed death longer than we have postponed disease, and this has been in one sense a Faustian bargain:

> In the elderly, eliminating CHD (coronary heart disease) and in particular sudden death would necessarily increase the number of fatalities ascribable to several other disorders of senescence such as Alzheimer's and Parkinson's diseases. If CHD can be wiped out, large numbers of perceived desirable deaths will be converted into much less appealing exits.[6]

This puts us in a sad and difficult situation. Health status declines with increasing age for virtually every health problem. An aging society will likely have more chronic disease and disability just because of the increasing population of older individuals. At the same time, we have invented, discovered, and researched ourselves into a new and challenging public policy dilemma by largely abolishing all the cheap and easy ways to die. The good news is that we have added almost thirty years to human life expectancy. We no longer die of infectious diseases such as typhoid, tuberculosis, and pneumonia. The bad news is that we die later but of more horrible illnesses.

We have saved ourselves from infectious diseases only to die of heart disease, cancer, and Alzheimer's. We have done a wonderful job of curing acute disease only to throw ourselves into the arms of chronic disease. Jeff Goldsmith reminds us that an acute disease is like an auto accident: two cars bang together, after which we take them into an auto repair shop called a hospital. A chronic disease is like a rusting car: the parts simply wear out. We are genetically programmed to do so. There is no cure for old age. We can postpone death, but death is inevitable. Chronic and degenerative diseases are the predominant health issues of the elderly and are increasing with an aging society.

An aging society—one exploding with technology, whose average worker has had only a small increase in real wages over the last thirty years, and which has failed to moderate the geometric increase in healthcare costs—has to start talking about how to allocate its scarce financial resources. We may be healthier longer, but we are still more and more expensive as we grow older.

# The Crime of the Century

I HAVE JUST PARTICIPATED IN THE GREATEST EMBEZZLEMENT IN ALL OF HISTORY. IN MY 60-plus years, I have never seen such a perfect crime. Like most other master criminals, I am heady with success and feel a need to brag. I kid you not; never before has one group appropriated as much money that belonged to another group in the history of crime. The victims, while they are increasingly suspicious, still do not know they have been had. It was literally and figuratively as easy as taking candy out of the mouths of babes.

Here is how we did it: The first rule of embezzlement is to find some naive patsy. We sensed nearly forty years ago that the younger generation was not paying enough attention to public policy, so we quietly found ways to maintain our lifestyles and charge it to the next generation. While those of you 50 years old and younger were preoccupied with other things, my generation dumped the largest load of debt on you that history has ever seen.

A good scam needs a compassionate come-on. In our case, we developed a new term, *poor elderly*. To this day, most Americans do not understand that this is actually two words and that *poor* no longer describes the elderly as a class. There are, of course, poor elderly, but as a class, the elderly have the most discretionary income of any group in America (except those in the age bracket of 55–65).

Next, we devised a number of systems that allowed us to charge our retirement to the next generation of Americans, who will wake up to find they are on the losing side of a Ponzi scheme. Like all good con artists, we relied on trust. We told them there was a trust fund for both Social Security and Medicare. Of course, this was a lie. There is no trust fund, in the normal sense of the word, because we take this month's Social Security taxes from today's workers and pay them to today's elderly.

Then we tell today's workers not to worry—the money is being held in trust. In actual fact (as Senator Ernest Hollings of South Carolina has observed), they would be no better off if the fund was invested in Confederate war bonds. The trust fund is a sham because it contains only IOUs that tomorrow's generation of workers will have to (mostly) pay off themselves. They will have to pay for both our retirement and their own. Not bad. We succeeded in taking money from poor workers in Saint Paul and sending it to wealthy retirees in Saint Petersburg—and no one was the wiser. But I have hardly begun.

The perfect embezzlement maximizes its take. We soon found there was money left over after paying the Social Security funds to today's elderly, and we did not want to stop halfway. Would a self-respecting crook leave money lying in the bank vault after a robbery? Hell no. We completed the job with something called the consolidated budget. This allowed us to quietly take the Social Security funds left over to reduce our taxes by spending the money on current government services. Under the consolidated budget, we could legally borrow the money in the trust fund left over every year and spend it on current government services, thereby reducing our yearly taxes.

Virtually every year for the last half-century or so, we understated both the yearly deficit and the total federal debt. Even though the official federal debt is approximately $15 trillion, the amount actually passed on to the next generation is closer to $80–$100 trillion. Members of my generation are master embezzlers. The entire scheme was done with clever accounting gimmicks, which allowed us to minimize our taxes and maximize our spending while we passed the bill on to the next generation. By the time they, like many victims of a crime, figure it out, I will be long gone.

I have completely and totally spent the Social Security Trust Fund and left nothing in trust, absolutely nothing, for today's workers to pay future obligations. They will have to either raise their taxes substantially or dramatically reduce their benefits under the system. They have no other practical alternatives. They may, of course, try to do the same thing that my generation did and try to perpetrate the Ponzi scheme, but I doubt it will work. Young people catch on at some point. The true perfect crime only works once.

The next generation will wake up to the magnitude of the fraud. They will recognize they are working long hours (or two jobs) and make less working than I make in retirement. Yet every month, they transfer money to me to pay for my health benefits. I have plans for that also. When they start to blow the whistle, I will say with shock and horror, "You can't start an intergenerational war." I will tell them about how hard I fought for this country (six months in active service—most of it at the officers' club bar). I will shame them by accusing them of breaking the generational contract, neatly covering the fact that it was really my generation who broke the contract by leaving them an unsustainable and insolvent system. Like any successful crook, I will cover all my bases.

When healthcare costs became a larger factor in our budgets, we found a system to subsidize our healthcare costs at the expense of following generations. We called it Medicare. The average couple who turned 65 in 2010 got back three dollars from today's workers for every one dollar that was paid into the system. That couple will receive, on the average, a $241,000 subsidy toward their healthcare costs—from a system that is slated to go broke not far into this century. I am looking forward to playing golf and living high and sending much of the bill to today's workers who make less working full-time than I make in retirement. *Après moi, le deluge.*

The story does not end there. My generation screwed up the savings and loan industry. What did we do to get out of it? We issued thirty-year bonds! Why should I pay for my mistakes when there is a gullible generation right behind me? Will I be here in thirty years? No. Will you? I leave it to my kids to pay off.

My wife and I bought our first house in 1963 for $11,900. Our first mortgage payments were $49 a month because we had a VA loan subsidized by the federal government. Everyone in my generation could buy his or her own home. It is estimated that 30 percent of the current workers below age 30 will never be able to own their own houses. But there's more. To this day, I get more money in housing allowance every year from the federal government than the poorest American. It is simple. I get to deduct my mortgage interest and real estate taxes, which is worth to someone in my income bracket more than the cash equivalent that any poor person in this state receives for housing. Ditto health benefits. By not taxing my health insurance paid for by my employer, the federal government provides me more health benefits than it does most poor children on Medicaid.

Do I feel guilty? Well, occasionally. The other night I was standing in the line for the movies, getting a senior citizen discount. The struggling young couple in front of me were wondering how they were going to pay the babysitter. My wife and I had driven to the theater in our fancy foreign car from our debt-free house, but we got a six-dollar discount from the price the young couple paid.

I try not to spend too much time thinking about it. I keep busy. Right now, I have to go down to the state legislature to lobby for free fishing licenses for seniors. Why not? We already get free state park admission. See you around.

## Demography Basics

Understanding the current and future needs surrounding healthcare requires a closer examination of demographic estimates and projections. Given a comprehensive body of research in numerous health services journals suggesting elderly disproportionately use health services, a practical approach in controlling healthcare costs may be to better understand the changing elderly population and its needs. To expound, examine the following population pyramids:

**FIGURE 1.** POPULATION PYRAMIDS BY AGE AND GENDER 1980–2020

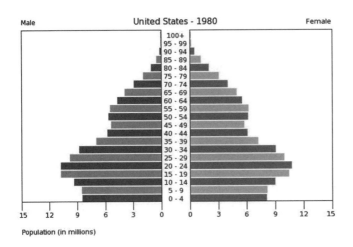

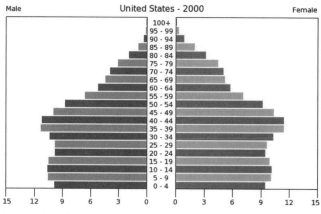

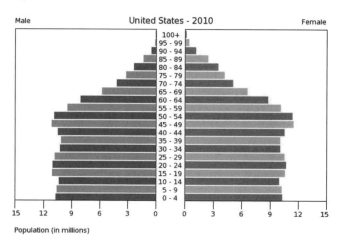

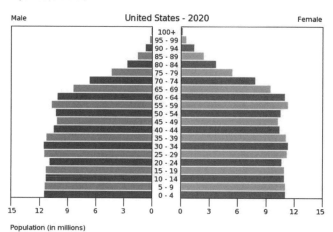

*Source:* Data from US Bureau of the Census

Demographers frequently utilize population pyramids to understand age and cohort dynamics. Population pyramids show the number of individuals in five-year age groups, starting from 0–4 years all the way to 100+. By recognizing the aging of each cohort (as well as the fertility and mortality rate), one can project the future population. This population structure may be growing, stable, stationary, or contracting. A growing or expanding structure appears triangular with a large base and narrow top. In this instance, children represent a large segment of the population. This type of population pyramid suggests a high birthrate as well as a high death rate (see below illustrations). A stable structure, as the name implies, maintains an unchanging fertility and mortality rate while a stationary structure maintains low fertility and mortality. The stationary pyramid appears like half an ellipse. Finally, we have the contracting structure. In this instance, children represent a smaller segment of the population. This type of population pyramid suggests a low birthrate and a low death rate.

**FIGURE 2.** GROWING POPULATION STRUCTURE

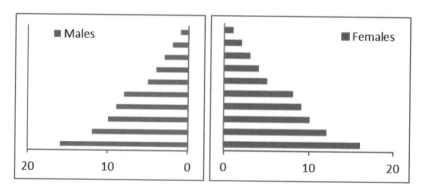

**FIGURE 3.** CONTRACTING POPULATION STRUCTURE

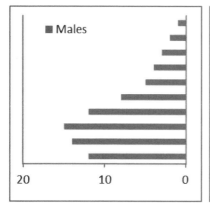
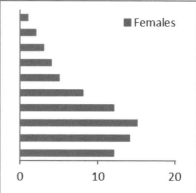

For the United States, we have a population structure with nearly equal representation at many age groups and a growing representation at older age groups. From 1980 to 2010, the percentage of the population age 65 and over has been steadily increasing, and this is expected to continue into 2020. This phenomenon has been called the graying of America. Naturally, one might ask, What caused this? or Why did this occur? The increasing proportion of elderly can be attributed to the baby boom generation and longer life spans. In our context, a baby boomer is any individual born between 1946 and 1964. This cohort represents a large segment of the population because many soldiers were returning home after World War II, getting married, and starting families. As the below illustration shows, the birthrate skyrocketed after 1940 and remained at a high level for nearly two decades.

**FIGURE 4.** HISTORICAL BIRTH RATES

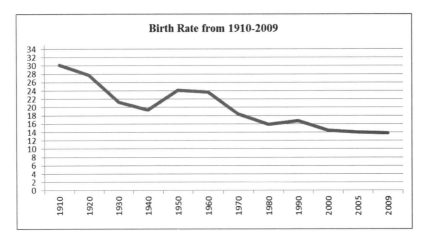

*Source:* Data from US Department of Health and Human Services, National Center for Health Statistics

In 2011, the first wave of baby boomers reached the retirement age of 65. The United States will experience a steady growth in this age group for the next few decades. And with increasing life spans, the older age groups will represent nearly 20 percent of the population. To understand this growth, consider the following statistics from historical US Census reports:

**FIGURE 5.** NUMBER AND PERCENTAGE OF POPULATION AGE 65 AND OVER

| YEAR | 1900 | 1940 | 1980 | 2010 |
|---|---|---|---|---|
| Population # | 3,080,498 | 9,019,314 | 25,549,427 | 40,267,984 |
| Population % | 4.1 | 6.8 | 11.3 | 13.0 |

*Source:* Data from US Bureau of the Census

During the past century, our elderly population has multiplied by a factor of thirteen and the percentage has more than tripled. This demographic change is noteworthy not only from an economic and social viewpoint but also with respect to healthcare. A recent article in the *New England Journal of Medicine* by

Dr. Susan Okie asserts, "As baby boomers enter their 60s, their increasing medical needs combined with a worsening shortage of primary care doctors are expected to fuel a crisis in healthcare for the elderly." Citing 2005 data from the Institute of Medicine, Okie provides some compelling statistics. For example, the number of physician visits per 100 people equals 329 for all ages. For those age 65–74, this number is a staggering 647, and 768 for those 75 and over. As for number of days of hospital care per 100 people, this approximates 55.4 for all ages, 139.8 for 65–74, and 259.4 for 75 and over.

## Key Statistics for the Elderly

THE 2010 US CENSUS SHOWS APPROXIMATELY 13 PERCENT OF THE US POPULATION are age 65 and over. Of that age group, not surprisingly, approximately 57 percent are female and 43 percent are male. Historically, this has not always been the case. In the first part of the twentieth century, males actually outnumbered females at older ages, but this trend reversed after the 1930s, with females coming to represent a much larger share.

FIGURE 6. NUMBER OF MALES AND FEMALES AGE 65 AND OVER

| YEAR | 1900 | 1940 | 1980 | 2010 |
|---|---|---|---|---|
| Males | 1,555,418 | 4,406,120 | 10,304,915 | 17,362,960 |
| Females | 1,525,080 | 4,613,194 | 15,244,512 | 22,905,024 |

Source: Data from US Bureau of the Census

Interestingly, when we compare the number of males to the number of females using the male-to-female ratio, both the 2000 and 2010 US Census show a slight increase in the male-to-female ratio. The below graphics depict the ratio of males to females for the 65-and-over age group from 1900 to 2010.

**FIGURE 7.** MALE TO FEMALE RATIO FOR 65-AND-OVER AGE GROUP

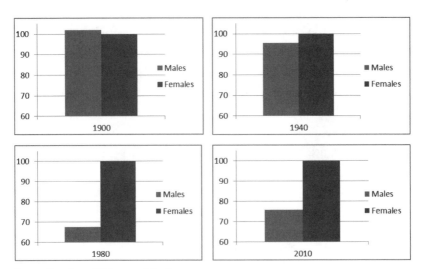

Source: Data from US Bureau of the Census

By and large, males are outnumbered in the 65-and-over age category because females live longer. The most recent estimates from the World Health Organization list 76 years and 80.9 years for male and female life expectancy at birth, respectively.[7]

## Disability

THE *2008 DISABILITY STATUS REPORT: THE UNITED STATES* BY WILLIAM ERIKSON, Camille G. Lee, and Sarah von Schrader (Cornell University) shows that for all age groups under 75, males have higher disability rates than females. And at younger ages, males have a rate that is nearly double. In the age group 21–64, the disparity is extremely small. At the 75-and-over group, there is a reversal—the female rate is *greater* by approximately 4 percent (males at 49.1 percent and females at 53.1 percent).

**FIGURE 8.** DISABILITY PREVALENCE RATES: GENDER AND AGE (%)

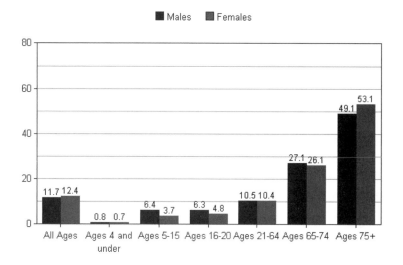

*Source:* W. Erikson, C. Lee, & S. von Schrader (2012). **2010 Disability Status Report: United States. Ithaca, NY: Cornell University Employment and Disability Institute (EDI).**

Another perspective is that of the nearly 10.5 million women age 75 and over in 2008, more than 5.5 million were maintaining some type of disability. To get to the heart of the matter, elderly women are more likely to suffer from disabilities. Women are also more likely to live in this condition of disability as widows since they live an average of nearly five additional years. This is important to recognize because disability is associated with greater healthcare expenditures and greater levels of formal and informal caregiving. By recognizing disability and life-expectancy differentials, we may be better able to control healthcare costs and improve population health by targeting health policies toward younger women. For example, encouraging routine checkups for bone density, blood pressure, diabetes, and vision/hearing (in addition to pap smears and mammograms) could halt the progression of and even reverse some age-related conditions. In short, an ounce of prevention is worth a pound of cure. Much of this is succinctly captured by Jeff Williamson and Marco Pahor in the *Archives of Internal Medicine.* These scholars examined numerous articles investigating the benefits of exercise and suggest that "it is also now well established that higher quantities of physical activity have beneficial effects on numerous age-related conditions such as osteoarthritis, falls and hip fracture, cardiovascular disease, respiratory diseases, cancer, diabetes mellitus, osteoporosis, low fitness and obesity, and decreased functional capacity."[8]

## Health and Education

IN A 2010 ISSUE OF *JOURNAL OF HEALTH ECONOMICS*, SCHOLARS DAVID CUTLER and Adriana Lleras-Muney undertake a rigorous inquiry into health and education (i.e., exploring the causal mechanisms of education), employing six unique data sets to understand the health education gradient. The below table provides a summary of their key findings.

**FIGURE 9.** SHARE OF EDUCATION GRADIENT EXPLAINABLE BY DIFFERENT FACTORS

| Factor | Explanatory power | | | | | |
|---|---|---|---|---|---|---|
| | NHIS | HRS | NLSY | MIDUS | NCDS | Approximate summary |
| Economic resources | 32% | 17% | 12% | 11% | 24% | 20% |
| Additional reduction when add: | | | | | | |
| Specific knowledge | 12% | NA | NA | NA | NA | 12% |
| Cognitive ability | NA | NA | 15% | NA | 44% | 30% |
| Tastes | NA | 0% | NA | 1% | 2% | 1% |
| Personality | 4% | NA | 4% | 1% | 2% | 3% |
| Social integration | NA | NA | NA | 7% | 15% | 11% |

**NHIS: National Health Interview Survey**
**HRS: Health and Retirement Study**
**NLSY: National Longitudinal Survey of Youth**
**MIDUS: Midlife Development in the US**
**NCDS: National Childhood Development Study**

*Source:* Reprinted from *Journal of Health Economics,* vol. 29, no. 1, David M. Cutler and Adriana Lleras-Muney, "Understanding Differences in Health Behaviors by Education," 1–28, © 2010, with permission from Elsevier.

Cutler and Lleras-Muney suggest that economic resources, such as income and health insurance, are important and account for nearly 20 percent of the gradient. The health education gradient is further explained by cognitive ability. These scholars state, "Our most surprising result is that education seems to influence cognitive ability, and cognitive ability in turn leads to healthier behaviors. As far as we can tell, the impact of cognitive ability is not so much what one knows, but how one processes information." Their results also show that specific knowledge and social integration can play a pivotal role: "what is learned from age 7 to 11, and then from age 11 to 16 accounts for a significant portion of the education gradient."

Given this and other research, how would we answer the question, Can greater education improve health? With a resounding yes. By providing basic health education as early as kindergarten and then reinforcing this during elementary, middle, and high school, we may achieve a population with better general health. In the process, we may also reduce health disparities and be in a position to manage some of our healthcare costs.

## Health and Income

THE HEALTH AND INCOME GRADIENT HAS ALSO BEEN WIDELY STUDIED. IN A 2002 article in *Health Affairs*, Angus Deaton asks if redistributing income would improve population health. This is a reasonable question given a large and substantial body of research that shows individuals with greater income tend to have better health and longer life spans. Should we target the poor or particular social groups or specific diseases in order to achieve a population with better health?

A recent article in the *American Journal of Public Health* by Paula A. Braveman et al. continues this line of research by examining health indicators and socioeconomic disparities for children and adults. Their results suggest that a gradient pattern *is* evident. Specifically, "Those with the lowest income and who were least educated were consistently less healthy, but for most indicators, even groups with intermediate income and education levels were less healthy than the wealthiest and most educated." The below graphs summarize some of their key findings. In the first graph, individuals with greater income (400 percent above the federal poverty line) maintain a longer life span at age 25, and this holds across *all* racial groups. The second graph shows individuals with greater income have lower rates of diabetes in the 20–64 age group, all else equal. Once again, this holds across *all* racial groups.

**FIGURE 10.** INCOME DISPARITIES IN ADULT HEALTH (LIFE EXPECTANCY) AND DIABETES

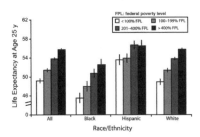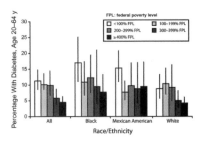

**FPL: federal poverty level**

*Source:* P. A. Braveman, C. Cubbin, S. Egerter, D. R. Williams, and E. Pamuk, "Socioeconomic Disparities in Health in the United States: What the Patterns Tell Us," *American Journal of Public Health*, vol. 100, no. S1, S193, © 2010, with permission from The Sheridan Press.

On the heels of these results, Braveman et al. offer an interesting perspective, suggesting that policies should address both the most socially disadvantaged and intermediate groups. Such an approach may gain wider political support.

Given this research, one might argue for redistribution of income. However, simply giving more money would not necessarily reduce health disparities and control healthcare costs. Instead of redistributing income or engineering welfare-related programs, a more practical approach may be to shift spending toward education, particularly for the poor. Greater investment in human capital could also result in higher incomes.

# The Corner Place with Governor Lamm

## *Thoughts on Intergenerational Equity*

I GRADUATED FROM HIGH SCHOOL IN 1953, AND I INHERITED FROM MY PARENTS A small federal debt and the world's largest creditor nation. I am leaving my children a staggering federal debt and the world's largest debtor nation.

I inherited an exporting nation with a high saving rate, and I'm leaving my children an importing nation with a dramatically lower saving rate. I inherited a nation that produced more than it consumed, and I'm leaving my kids a nation that consumes more than it produces.

Successful democracy, in the long run, requires some allegiance to and respect for the future. In the short run, modern public financing gives public policy makers incredible opportunities to encumber the future for present political gain:

1. My generation of politicians has relentlessly and quietly encumbered the nation's future earnings. Compare the federal debt to our gross domestic product:

| Year | Federal Debt | GDP |
|------|-------------|-----|
| 1981 | $1 trillion | $3 trillion |
| 1986 | $2 trillion | $4 trillion |
| 1992 | $4 trillion | $6 trillion |
| 1997 | $5.4 trillion | $7 trillion |
| 2003 | $6.5 trillion | $11 trillion |
| 2008 | $10.0 trillion | $13.2 trillion |
| 2011 | $15.0 trillion | $15.2 trillion |

In times of great prosperity, we have quietly increased the debt as a percentage of the GDP. And every year we dramatically understate the yearly deficit by offsetting the real deficit with money borrowed from some 150 federal trust funds (such as the Social Security Trust Fund). The total of the published annual deficits for the ten years of the nineties is approximately $1 trillion, but the actual federal debt has increased more than $4 trillion. In other words, the yearly deficit is not the real amount we add to the debt for that year; it is considerably understated. My generation has not been honest with the public.

2. We have dramatically understated the total federal debt. The total amount of federal debt, which we say we are leaving the future generation, is close to $15 trillion, but that in no way represents the cost of government services, which my generation enjoyed but leave to the following generation to pay off.

We have to honestly compute the true costs of the future starting with the unfunded liabilities, which, I argue, make the real federal debt that our children will have to pay off for services enjoyed by my generation far closer to $80–$100 trillion. Military retirement, federal civil service retirement, and Social Security payments are all owed for which no (or inadequate) money has been set aside. There is a whole category of government services that we enjoyed but that we left our kids the bill to pay. Fiscal fraud, clearly.

3. We have also told the public that the Social Security Trust Fund is an asset, but it is not; there is nothing there that will help future taxpayers pay off future Social Security payments. The trust fund owns nothing but US government bonds that our kids will have to raise the money to pay. Future taxpayers will thus inherit a large amount of federal government bonds that they will have to pay themselves. We don't even pay the interest on those bonds but instead pay the interest by selling additional federal bonds that they will also have to pay.

If we would have bought bonds or stocks of another country, there would be value in the fund, for the debt would be on their taxpayers. But we bought US government bonds and essentially added this debt to the national credit card. We have been credit card liberals: there has been no program that we didn't consider worthy of funding and then putting on the national credit card. We knew what we wanted, but not what we could afford. We have enriched our own political careers by voting for myriad programs that we couldn't pay for. We get the political benefit; the future gets the bill. Great deal for me, terrible deal for public policy, and a tragic legacy to leave to our children.

One of the great issues of the future will be intergenerational equity when the younger generations start to recognize what we have done to them. My generation lived in the afterglow of the New Deal. We misread Keynes and thought that borrowing, because it worked in the thirties and forties, could continue forever. But we found that debt is economic cocaine; it is very hard to stop borrowing once you start. Every generation should pay for the government services it uses. Robert Louis Stevenson said, "Sooner or later, we all sit down to a banquet of consequences." True, except my generation of politicians will not be sitting there when the bills become due. We have been good neighbors but bad ancestors.

## The Medicare and Social Security Trust Funds Are Illusions!

WE ARE COMMITTING A FRAUD ON OUR CHILDREN AND GRANDCHILDREN. WE ARE TELLing them that the Medicare and Social Security Trust Funds will help them fund their Medicare and Social Security benefits when they, in turn, retire. But these so-called trust funds are not assets for the next generation; they are instead accounting gimmicks that have no real value to our children. There are no current savings backing up these trust funds. Our children will have to pay all their Medicare and Social Security spending out of their income stream. We have left them nothing of value in these trust funds.

Our children will essentially inherit an accounting wash, i.e., government bonds (an asset) and the obligation to pay off those bonds (a liability). There is no inherent value to the trust funds because our generation spent all the money. We took in FICA taxes and spent them on (1) current social benefits and (2) other government services for ourselves. Every cent. Every year we have been spending all the FICA taxes we take in. Our children will have to either cut spending, increase taxes, or reborrow the money. They will get no real monetary value from this misnamed fund.

If you inherit a million dollars in government bonds, you are a million dollars richer. All Americans owe you and are legally obligated to pay you face value of those bonds plus interest. If your generation inherits a trillion dollars of government bonds, you have inherited nothing of value. My generation spent the money and has left our children an accounting entry without real value. We even pay the interest on those bonds by giving our children more bonds, which they in turn must pay.

*The Economist* magazine said of the trust funds, "It is as if an indebted person had put aside a little nest egg of savings consisting entirely of IOUs signed by himself." The Medicare and Social Security Trust Funds consist of IOUs, which our children will have to pay off. Observe: if we were to double these funds or even triple them, there would be no increase in value to the next generation. They would have to raise the money to pay off double the amount of bonds. Double this asset and you also double the liability we impose on the future.

Dorcas Hardy, former commissioner of Social Security, has said, "There are no trust funds, just a bunch of IOUs." She goes on:

> The government would have us believe that Social Security is accumulating huge trust funds that will be used in the twenty-first century to help finance the high cost of retirement benefits that will become payable. This simply is not true. Present funds, and probably future funds, are mere window dressing and have no economic reality.

The Congressional Research Service's report to Congress of January 27, 1991, concedes that the government uses all of the trust funds for general purposes and that all the Social Security system has is a promise by the government to repay the bonds. "Perhaps the biggest misconception is that the social security trust funds represent actual resources to be used for future benefit payments, rather than what is in reality a promise by Government to take steps necessary to secure resources from the economy at that time."

David Wessel of *The Wall Street Journal* has said, "It's akin to a father putting money into an old cigar box for his young daughter's college education at the beginning of every week, taking it out at the end of the week to pay the light bills, and replacing the cash with his IOUs."

The Medicare and Social Security surpluses are extra taxes we are collecting today from all workers—to spend today on our needs—and to imply that these bonds in the Social Security and Medicare Trust Funds will help our children is an Orwellian distortion. They represent excess taxes being collected now and spent now, leaving whatever amounts are in the trust fund to be paid by our children. We get the benefit; they get the bill.

If these funds would invest in German bonds, then the trust funds would be real assets. The German public would have the obligation, and our children would have true assets to help them offset their own obligations.

But there are no assets or investments in the funds of the type that would help our children pay future benefits. Ask yourself, how will the next generation get the money to redeem the bonds and thereby pay the Medicare and Social Security benefits then due? The government will have to collect the revenue because the trust fund contains nothing of value that they can use to pay benefits when due. Our children will have to raise taxes, cut spending, or reborrow the money. The trust funds do not reduce by one penny the fiscal obligations of future generations.

## The Book Nook with Dr. Sharma

### Thoughts on Health and Education

THERE EXISTS A WIDE BODY OF RESEARCH SHOWING A POSITIVE ASSOCIATION BETWEEN education and health, all other things being equal. Readers interested in undertaking a preliminary and historical approach to this connection should start by examining some books by James C. Riley. A significant part of Riley's work focuses on population, government, and health. His book *Rising Life Expectancy: A Global History* examines how different approaches to public health, medicine, wealth, nutrition, behavior, and education have been used to reduce mortality and increase life expectancy. In addition, *Poverty and Life Expectancy: The Jamaica Paradox* highlights increased education and public health interventions as practical and useful tools in reducing mortality. Riley suggests that community health campaigns and, in particular, parental education regarding disease prevention can markedly increase life expectancy. Such an approach has been used with a degree of success in many lesser-developed countries. What about the United States? Can greater education improve health—more specifically, education focusing on the benefits of nutrition, physical activity, and dental hygiene? Would such investments in education be practical for those below the poverty line? Equally important, can such an approach help contain healthcare costs?

**FIGURE 11.** FRACTION OF THE OBSERVED DISPARITIES IN OUTCOMES DUE TO EDUCATION

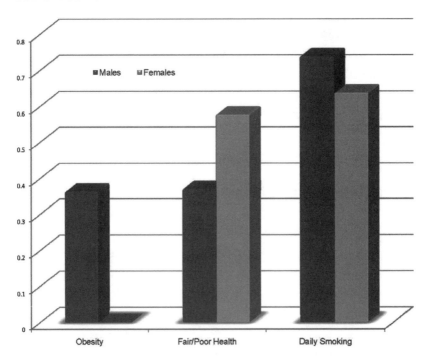

*Source:* Gabriella Conti and James Heckman, "Understanding the Early Origins of the Education-Health Gradient," *Perspectives on Psychological Science,* vol. 5, no. 5, p 21, © 2010. Reprinted by permission of SAGE Publications.

Before examining these questions, let's consider research by Gabriella Conti and Nobel laureate James J. Heckman. These scholars suggest that cognitive and health endowments developed as early as age 10 are important determinants of health disparities by age 30.[9] The above figure shows differences in health that can be attributed to education. For example, according to Conti and Heckman, education "plays an important role in explaining differences in smoking behavior [and] a much more important role in accounting for the gap in obesity rates for males than it does for females." A nearly 0.7 fraction of the health disparity can be explained by education for men and a nearly 0.6 for women for daily smoking, all else equal. Although the impact is not as high, education also impacts self-reported health (middle bars). This research also shows the importance of taking gender into account when examining health disparities. Conti and Heckman use these findings to suggest that the early years are crucial in health promotion and prevention.

## Individual Choice, Incentives, and Intervention

I AM A POLICY ANALYST WHO BELIEVES IN USING ECONOMIC TOOLS TO ADDRESS PUBLIC issues. I support and believe in individual choice—and that requires full information (or near full) on the part of consumers. This information can be acquired through education and experience. There exists a large body of research, including the aforementioned titles, that recognizes the importance of education in promoting health. If individuals take it upon themselves to allocate a few hours per week to reading health magazines, examining online health letters, attending health seminars, or even watching credible television programs focusing on health issues, then we could improve population health and possibly control a small fraction of healthcare costs. Of course, what one does with this education is just as important. In chapter 3, Rebuilding the House of Healthcare, I discuss novel approaches utilized by IBM to engage employees in healthier lifestyles. This is an example of where *incentives* can be very useful. There is much the business community can do to improve employee health and morale while simultaneously finding simple ways to reduce healthcare costs. This is also an example of individuals being rewarded for applying newly acquired skills and concepts.

Although I do not believe government intervention should necessarily be the first tool to address some public issues, there is a role for local and state government. As Conti and Heckman highlight, investments in early education are worthwhile. In other words, early education can yield a high rate of return on health. Perhaps our early education system should provide instruction on oral hygiene and *not* leave this to annual dental visits, which some children do not even receive. Perhaps our early education system should provide instruction on simple ways to increase physical activity, easy ways to add more whole foods to a daily diet, and even how to use meditation to reduce stress. Health should be part of the core curriculum as early as kindergarten. Much like reading, writing, and arithmetic, we need to consider health as an education fundamental. We simply cannot rely on annual visits or checkups for most of our health information. This knowledge needs to be disseminated more regularly and at younger ages. Equally important, we need to structure incentives to promote healthier lifestyles, whether through public or private intervention. This should be one focus area for public policy regarding healthcare.

# TWO

# "The Problem": Thinking about the US Healthcare System

## Healthcare and Policy

HEALTHCARE HAS BEEN THE FASTEST-GROWING COST OF BUSINESS, GOVERNMENT, AND the family budget. The explosive upward thrust of healthcare costs is and has been at the heart of most personal bankruptcies and labor disputes. The average American pays twice as much for his healthcare as he pays for all services of state government. After a few short years of leveling off, healthcare costs zoomed back to double-digit yearly increases, only to unexpectedly drop in 2011.

Yet we have every reason to think that costs will accelerate as the baby boomers retire and medical technology performs its expensive miracles. The first baby boomer turned 65 in 2011 and became eligible for Medicare. Medicare becomes insolvent not long after, and a river of red ink is projected as the bulk of the baby boomers move into retirement. The official projections may well be low; some health economists (e.g., Victor Fuchs) project that healthcare spending could average as high as $25,000 (1996 constant dollars) per senior citizen by 2020. It is hard to see how this will be affordable under any economic scenario.

It is important to recognize, amidst this litany of problems, that healthcare in America has been an incredible success. Caring health professionals have developed an infinite array of benefits to help us grow older. My generation of doctors and scientists has developed the most technological, competent healthcare in all of history. The bad news is that this is very expensive, it too often substitutes technology for other healthier strategies, and it misses many Americans.

It is commonly understood that medical technology and the aging of America are two important drivers of healthcare costs, but even more central are the expectations of the American public. Expectations are the fuel that drives many of the costs in healthcare. We are a creative can-do people who have come to expect what no nation can possibly deliver: all the healthcare that is (or may be) beneficial to our health. We read of a new advance in Monday's newspaper and feel entitled to it by Tuesday morning. America's essential healthcare dilemma is that we want more healthcare as worried patients than we are willing to pay for as tightfisted premiums payers or taxpayers.

One of the reasons for this unrealistic and unsustainable illusion is that Americans are mostly insulated from the full impact of these costs. More than 80 percent of US healthcare is paid for by third parties, either insurance or government, and what we don't pay for directly we tend to undervalue. We pay, of course, but we pay indirectly, either through taxes or through lower wages in the workplace. Approximately 17 percent of US healthcare costs are paid out of pocket. We feel no real economic impact for most healthcare transactions. Few of us have any idea of the cost of the healthcare we consume. "Health insurance coverage is seen as a credit card whose charges never come due, and 'more' care was always 'better' care," says health expert William Mercer.

Americans do not take easily to the concept of limits. But we must recognize that our curing and caring has the potential to force too many limited dollars into healthcare and also to financially break individual healthcare institutions:

> So long as all the physician had to offer the patient was his own time and advice and a few herbs and powders, both medicine and society could comfortably claim that the physician's duty of fidelity was owed solely to the individual patient.

When physicians can, with the stroke of their pens, literally bankrupt the community, the community may no longer be able to tolerate that view of the physician's duty.[1]

But it is reality time in America. No public or private expenditure can grow for very long at twice the rate of inflation. Government, chiefly in the form of Medicare and Medicaid, now funds nearly 45 percent of US healthcare. We could say that in a sense we have half-socialized medicine in America. There is near unanimity among policy experts that these governmental financing systems must be substantially amended. Not long ago, entitlement programs had 13 workers per retiree but are down to 3.3 workers per retiree today and may fall to as little as 2 workers as the baby boomers retire, having replaced themselves with far fewer children than their parents. Public policy faces a dilemma that is unprecedented in recent US history; we are going to have to take back benefits previously promised to the American public. There can hardly be a less-appealing task for politicians.

Almost every aspect of America's medicine is inflationary. One health policy expert coined the term *medical uncertainty principle,* where a patient's anxiety and a health worker's professionalism always urge more and more marginal healthcare to the point of absurdity. Our litigation system essentially imposes a lawyer tax on the entire healthcare system. So many pressures in the healthcare system, including the American tradition of individualism, drive unnecessary or marginal spending. The healthcare tradition has been developed with a focus on the individual patient and, as author Larry Churchill has noted, "is undergirded by a moral tradition which systematically excludes reference to the larger society."

No matter how we organize and fund healthcare, we will find that our medical miracles have outpaced our ability to pay. It is hard to change our thinking after years of blank-check medicine, but it is necessary. Limits are painful but unavoidable. We are investing in the unaffordable and spending the unsustainable. We need to focus limited resources on where they will buy the most health for society.

The basic dilemma of American public policy is that we cannot do politically what we need to do economically to retire the baby boomers and remain an industrially competitive nation. Our political traditions and values came out of the 1950s and 1960s, when America was a massive wealth-producing machine. When I entered the Colorado legislature in 1967, America was doubling its per capita wealth every thirty years. Today, a similar figure is hard to arrive at because the average American earns only a few more dollars (adjusted for inflation) in 2000 than he or she did in 1973. The halcyon days when we could say yes to all reasonable needs is over. Being in government and balancing a budget today is like sleeping with a blanket that is too short; your shoulders get cold, and you pull the blanket up only to freeze your feet. My generation has not honestly faced the implications of the age wave about to hit America. We cannot solve problems that we don't talk about.

## The Best Healthcare System in the World?

WE ARE TOLD AD NAUSEAM THAT THE UNITED STATES HAS THE BEST HEALTHCARE SYSTEM in the world. I think that statement is false at the present time but could, with some national effort and focus, become true. I am excited about the potential but depressed that so few people challenge the hubris that self-awards our nation's healthcare system with the number one ranking. Unfortunately, that statement may say more about us as a civic society than it says about the actual healthcare system. In 2000, the World Health Organization rated the US healthcare system 37th in terms of efficiency among the 191 it evaluated. Americans brushed aside the criticism and never seriously considered the very strong reasons for the low rating. We have heard so often that we are the best that we believe it, but most evidence is to the contrary.

The stakes are high. The largest purchase the average American family will make in their lifetime is no longer their house, but their healthcare. Over the last thirty years, healthcare has also been the fastest-growing part of the average household budget.

National spending on healthcare averages approximately $8,000 per person per year. This is approaching an amount equal to what we spend on average for both food and housing. Put another way, if healthcare spending had grown at the same rate as the economy instead of growing at twice the rate of the economy, we would today be paying less than half what we actually pay for healthcare. And judging from other developed countries, if this money was spent thoughtfully, we could be just as healthy.

Citizens are perpetually (and appropriately) up in arms about state taxes. Yet they rarely question our health expenditure, which totals twice the amount taxpayers pay for all state services. The time has come to ask—and answer—some hard questions about how American healthcare dollars are actually being spent and what we as a society are getting for that expenditure.

To answer the question, Do we have the best healthcare system in the world, let us consider some analogous public policy situations. What if we were to claim that we had the best road system in the world, with beautiful, well-maintained freeways that stop at the boundaries of each city, while traffic is paralyzed by congestion and our traffic deaths are among the highest in the world?

Do we claim that we have the best public safety system in the world, with the most advanced equipment and the best-trained officers, yet 15 percent of our neighborhoods are unpatrolled, our crime rate is high by international standards, and juvenile crime is on the rise?

Suppose we were to claim that we have the best education system in the world, with modern facilities and brilliant teachers, yet our world standing in education is far below that of other nations, and we fail to educate a significant portion of our population?

If we were to make such claims in those contexts, we would rightly deserve the ridicule of any sensible person—and of the world—yet we believe that the same applies to our claims regarding our best-in-the-world healthcare system. We are clearly puffing our wares.

While there is virtually no question that in medical research, training, and technology no one surpasses the United States, most experts agree with Robert Blank's concise analysis of the situation:

Although there is no doubt that Americans have the most extensive range of sophisticated medical technology in the world, we fall well short of most other nations in health promotion, preventive medicine, and access to primary care. Health outcomes as measured by morbidity and mortality rates fail to reflect the vast expenditure differential with other nations. Something, therefore, is dreadfully wrong.[2]

How, then, do we correct it? What does constitute a good healthcare system? Let's look at the previously mentioned yardstick established by Victor Fuchs, who claims that a healthcare system should be evaluated by three criteria: (1) technology and training, (2) access by the population, and (3) outcomes. While the United States excels in technology and training, in the other two categories it falls far short of other developed nations.

Despite the enormous amount of resources and talents expended on healthcare—50 percent more spending than any other developed country—America has the most uninsured citizens and underinsured citizens in the developed world, and our citizens are less healthy than those in Europe, Canada, or Japan in some important health indicators.

It is important to recognize that brilliant doctors and advanced technology alone are not enough to produce an excellent system. Why? Because we can have the best individual healthcare without having the best healthcare system. Because a system is no better than the sum of all its parts, and a weak link anywhere weakens the system overall.

However brilliant our providers, however advanced our technology, unless these advantages are accessible to the majority of our citizens, and unless they actually improve the health of Americans overall, we have no legitimate basis for claiming that we have the best healthcare system in the world. A genuine right to make that claim can be earned only after the United States adopts and implements a meaningful and effective public policy of universal coverage and focuses its attention less on the narrower issue of how to provide healthcare to individuals and more on the broader issue of how to keep a nation healthy.

# Allocating Public Resources

OVER THE LAST HALF-CENTURY, WE HAVE GRADUALLY REPLACED A MAJOR PART OF PRI-vate funding of healthcare with public or taxpayer money. Taxes, mostly federal taxes, now pay for approximately half of the nation's total healthcare expenses. But public policy seldom asks, What are we getting for our money? Government may or may not run the healthcare system, but it must inevitably be concerned with the public health generally and clearly should be concerned about the value America gets for the $2.6 trillion a year (2010) it spends in total for healthcare, or the approximately $700 billion funded with public tax dollars.

All taxpayer monies must be allocated to the various functions of government by budgets. Taxpayer money is fungible, and a budget tells us what we value—its relative importance and priority vis-à-vis other public needs. Budgeting is a world of trade-offs where often all interests are left underfunded.

Not only have we dramatically increased the role of government in funding healthcare, but also American business has come to the conclusion that it cannot afford or tolerate blank-check medicine. Employee health costs have exploded, and employers have responded by reducing coverage and/or cutting benefits. Many employers have simply stopped healthcare as a benefit. Too often, rising costs and the recession have left them without any choice.

All publicly funded social goods must live within a budget. The public policy of a healthcare system on a budget cannot be the mirror of medical ethics developed under an open-ended funding system. We have socialized half of healthcare in America, and public spending on healthcare must be weighed and compared to all other public needs. Current medical ethics either allow or require a range of actions that make no moral sense when compared with other current social demands. Many of these treatments would never be funded if they had to be prioritized among other social needs. Medical ethics and culture, mostly developed in our low- or modest-technology past assuming no or few resource constraints, form a map to a world that no longer exists.

Public policy must consider the costs and benefits of all social needs and cannot exempt healthcare from scrutiny. Public policy cannot say, "I don't care how much our actions raise your taxes or premiums." There must be limits that one person's health demand can impose on his neighbor. Life is valuable, life has a very high value, but it cannot be priceless.

Where is the moral high ground in a society that cannot disconnect feeding tubes to people in a persistent vegetative state (PVS) but does not connect the working poor to basic health coverage? How can we allow such results as elderly patients with new hips or pacemakers die from summer heat because they lack a fan in their room? How can the system pay for everything in allopathic medicine and nothing in other areas that advance health?

Public policy doesn't have the luxury of individual advocacy. It has to choose among many worthwhile civic goals. However important medicine is to society, it does not have a monopoly on achieving health. The monomaniacal pursuit of healthcare can unknowingly interfere with the total health of society.

Government can never fund all the beneficial health services a caring, imaginative, and technologically advanced society can develop. Government refuses to set limits by pretending there are no limits. Politicians promise a Patient's Bill of Rights, which will reinforce these unreasonable expectations. Healthcare professionals, caught in a cyclone of change, have assumed that government would fund everything they needed for their patients. It was and still is a system without brakes.

The real moral agony in public policy is not the anencephalic infant (i.e., born with only a functioning brain stem), but it is leaving the working poor uncovered, trading off between funds for prevention and treatment, and fairly allocating between the young and the old and between healthcare and the nation's other social priorities. Much literature on medical ethics is irrelevant to the funding world of public policy decisions. Where is it written that medicine has a moral priority over all other societal needs?

No budget can tolerate open-ended demands. Budgets allocate limited funds and must be able to fund something without funding everything. This process will inevitably develop conflicts between the physician as patient advocate and the payer as advocate for the group. Every healthcare system or plan can reasonably do more things technically than it can reasonably fund.

Putting together a budget, public or private, is empirical not philosophical. It is more a matter of social policy than ethics. It is not only a matter of moral reasoning but also a question of resource allocation, where everything we do prevents us from doing something else. Budget needs are interrelated and interdependent. In the rough-and-tumble world of budgeting, nothing can be given an automatic priority, not even something as important as healthcare.

This is clearly a different dynamic than what exists in the physician-patient relationship. Cost must always be a consideration in budgeting. No society can pay for everything that is or may be beneficial to its citizens. Public policy cannot allow the public defender, or the state patrol, or the highway department to demand everything beneficial in their area of public policy because a life is at stake. None of our public needs exists in a vacuum, but all must be put in context with other civic needs.

Do we really want infants born only with functioning brain stems—unable to live naturally beyond a few days—surviving months without a brain? Do we want people living years in persistent vegetative states and terminally ill people in an intensive care unit (ICU), all consuming public resources desperately needed elsewhere, to make this a just and decent society? Public policy can't have one publicly funded social need without a budget competing with other social needs any more than a family can have one favored child among neglected brothers and sisters. Public policy is always built on the foundation of trade-offs necessitated by budgets.

We should now recognize that if public policy continues to base a system on today's medical ethics and culture, the sum total of all ethical medicine as now defined and practiced would (1) cause the healthcare system to fall under its own weight, (2) bankrupt the nation, and (3) create an unethical society where one sector—medicine—exists amidst general social squalor.

# How Do You Buy Health for Society?

ONE INEVITABLE RESULT OF MACROALLOCATION OF LIMITED RESOURCES IN OTHER COUNtries is that the focus shifts from the individual to the larger question, How do you best care for the health of society? Other nations have come to the commonsense conclusion that public policy spending ought to maximize a nation's health, not an individual's healthcare. Public funds should be spent in ways that maximize public goals. Inevitably, nations start to ask, What policies buy the most health for the most people?

Canada, for example, commissioned a 1991 study, *The Determinants of Health*, that examined which policies provided the most health for its citizens. The study was needed because "the fundamental reality of constrained resources, public or private, lies behind most, if not all, issues of healthcare policy. The principal task for most developed societies is to find ways of making more effective use of the resources now devoted to healthcare." That sums up clearly the chief challenge of every nation's search for health.

The study found that Canadians were spending too much on healthcare treatments and not enough on other health-enhancing activities. They were not maximizing the public resources; they were not asking hard-enough questions.

Researchers found that the clear evidence that there is more to health than healthcare had been largely ignored, despite the fact that increased spending on the formal healthcare system was "no longer having a correspondingly positive impact on the overall population's health." Canadians were spending more and more to achieve less and less health.

The study pointed out that spending money on the healthcare system was not the best way to a healthy society. It found: "The most dramatic historical improvements in the health of the average individual have been associated with increased prosperity. The enhanced prosperity of regions leads to better living and working conditions. It is the effect on the social environment that appears to have been key in changing the health status of the population."

The study urged Canadians to expand their concept of health far beyond medical care and to "adopt a new framework for understanding health. The challenge of the future lies in using this knowledge to develop effective policies that will ensure a healthy and prosperous society." The government of Canada now intends to give human biology, the environment, and lifestyle as much attention as it has to the financing of healthcare organizations so that all four avenues to improved health are pursued with equal vigor.

Similarly, in Great Britain, two famous reports, the Black Report (1982) and the Health Divide report (1992), both found that the inequalities in health showed too much reliance in Britain on a narrow and outmoded definition of health. The reports suggest a new kind of health policy needs to account for factors other than health services.

A similar dialogue is going on all over the developed world. How does a society produce health? The answer increasingly is that the healthcare system is only a part of the health agenda. Nations must start to focus on producing health, and this may involve saying no to aspects of individual healthcare. In fact, health may be best achieved in areas of social policy other than healthcare.

For instance, Archie Cochrane, a famous British physician, refused in 1972 to support more resources to Britain's National Health Service (NHS), observing there was more health in other (nonhealth) areas of social policy. "I have no intention of joining the clamor for far more money for the NHS. If more money becomes available for the welfare services, I think an increase in old-age pensions should have priority."

The fact that we added thirty years to human life expectancy last century has to do mostly with public policy and the public health profession, not the medical profession. We achieved most of our drop in mortality before we started spending vast amounts on the healthcare system. John B. McKinlay and Sonja M. McKinlay point out that "the introduction of specific medical measures and/or the expansion of medical services are generally not responsible for most of the modern decline in mortality."[3]

This theme is the standard opinion of scholars. It is widely held among health researchers; for instance, Laurene Graig writes, "Most research on the evolution of mortality trends suggest that improvements in such socioeconomic factors as education, income, nutrition, housing, sanitation and working conditions are, in combination, the primary determinants of health and mortality, not medical care."[4]

The US Department of Health and Human Services in its report *For a Healthy Nation 2000* states, "Clinical medicine, however, is credited with only five of the 30 years that have been added to life expectancy since the turn of the century."

In the United States we never ask, How do we spend our resources to achieve the most health? The results are tragic: too much spent on mainstream or allopathic medicine and too little spent on public health, too much spent on acute diseases and too little on chronic diseases, too much on rescue medicine and not enough on preventive medicine, and too many specialists and too few primary physicians. We need a larger vision of health than the leaders of healthcare have been giving us.

Arnold S. Relman, former editor of the *New England Journal of Medicine*, states:

> The public's health depends much more on genetic and cultural characteristics and environmental factors than on the quality of its medical care. . . . Physicians can diagnose disease and sometimes save or prolong life, particularly when the problem is acute. They can comfort and reassure patients and can relieve symptoms thereby improving the quality of life. But none of these services, valuable as they may be, is likely to affect the general level of the public's health as much as measures aimed at improving the social environment and behavior of people. To improve general life expectancy and infant mortality significantly, we need to improve the housing, education, and economic condition of our urban and rural poor. That task is beyond the reach of medicine.

It is our strong belief that we would be much healthier as a nation if we spent 9 to 10 percent of our GNP on healthcare and spent the additional 5 percent on public health, fighting smoking and obesity, educating, creating jobs, and raising the standard of living of the bottom 40 percent of the population. It is doubtful that we are getting our money's worth from the $2.3 trillion we spend on healthcare. American medicine looks at health narrowly. The practice of medicine is driven by forces that have very little to do with the ranking health needs of the population; it is preoccupied with sophisticated therapeutic interventions, which often have questionable benefits to the patients and society.

No matter how we organize healthcare and fund healthcare, we will find that our ability to discover medical miracles has outpaced our ability to pay for them. We shall need to focus limited resources on where they will buy the most health for society.

We are inventing the unaffordable and spending the unsustainable. We need to start discussing now what we can morally leave undone. This, according to Laurene Graig, is "a dilemma so new that neither our social, legal, and religious institutions, nor our healthcare providers or consumers, have developed a satisfactory way of coping." Yet cope we must.

Public policy can save more lives more cheaply than many of the fancy technologies with which we fill our hospitals. We need a larger vision of the concept of healthcare. A drunk-driving bill is healthcare. A sustained, publicly funded campaign against smoking and obesity could reduce mortality and morbidity as much or more than our nation could by curing cancer. One has to ask whether it makes sense to pour billions of dollars into a healthcare delivery system that is often effective only at the margin while forgoing these other much more effective policies that clearly save lives and health. Healthcare spending is a bottomless pit. Let's start asking some hard questions about how this money is spent.

## A Six-Count Indictment of US Healthcare

AMERICA HAS PAID A HEAVY PRICE FOR SPARE-NO-COST MEDICINE, AN INDIVIDUAL AT A time. We have almost lost touch with reality; we have insulated ourselves from the harsh inevitability of setting limits and priorities.

Our national culture, our medical ethics, our media-fueled expectations, and our hearts are still in an era of open-ended funding. We continue to act as if we do not have to make trade-offs and that by maximizing the health of individuals, we maximize the health of society. By our public policy negligence, we have indirectly helped fund excesses and ignored inadequacies that would simply not be tolerated in other sectors of government spending. Consider:

### 1. The Uninsured

A government pledged to equal protection and fairness is the chief funder of a healthcare system that leaves more than 50 million uninsured. By blindly funding healthcare according to providers' ethics, we have lost our public interest perspective and ignored completely the opportunity cost of those dollars. Mesmerized by medical technology, we fund some citizens excessively and leave others totally out of the insurance system. While some terminally ill people are kept alive at great expense, other Americans die for lack of basic services. Our total moral vision is dimmed because our focus is on the patient and not on the larger public policy goals. The patient advocate role is appropriate for a physician but inappropriate for those who purchase healthcare for a larger group. Public policy's patient is the entire society.

Perhaps even more seriously, we are ignoring what science and policy know about producing health for society, concentrating instead on allopathic medicine for individuals. We have ignored the wise warning of health economist Robert Evans that a society that spends too much on healthcare and not enough on other health-creating activities "may be actually reducing the health of its population through increased health spending."

### 2. The Elderly

Those citizens that government does cover are often covered because of their age, regardless of need, while others in need of health services go without. Medicaid does not cover approximately 50 percent of our medically indigent. We subsidize through Medicare many that could well afford to pay for their own healthcare. At the same time, we ignore many medically indigent Americans.

We tax our working poor (who often do not have health insurance themselves) to raise a pool of money, much of which goes to subsidize healthcare for those often richer than those we tax. Additionally, we tax workers who, even when they are insured, are predominately in managed care systems, and we use their money to fund fee-for-service medicine for the elderly. It is the political power of the elderly, not compassionate or thoughtful policy, that has guided our decisions.

### 3. The Public Policy of Health

By our obsessive search for health through medicine, we have ignored many important health-related services. We overfunded medicine and underfunded public health. We lacked the moral insight to see that public policy inevitably rations. We refused to see the bigger picture. Twenty-two million Americans went without needed dental care last year, and a number of quality-of-life needs were ignored in favor of doing everything in medicine. American hospitals have many more intensive care beds than the rest of the developed world, and yet our nation lacks adequate long-term care, home care services, or sufficient senior citizen centers. By funding the demands of medical need as interpreted by physicians for individual patients, we have created an ethically questionable public system.

### 4. The Specialists

Government has been the chief funder of a medical education system that has given us too many specialist physicians. Despite thirty years of warning by a variety of studies and commissions, physicians are dramatically overbalanced toward specialists. Great excess sits throughout America cheek by jowl with great need. We have overemphasized medicine and underemphasized health, overproduced specialists and underproduced primary healthcare providers.

### 5. Hospitals versus Schools

Government funding has helped to build an overcapacity into our health system infrastructure, which would never be tolerated in any other branch of government. Approximately one-third of

America's licensed hospital beds are empty, and we have a massive oversupply and duplication of medical technologies that are underutilized and inefficient, even by governmental standards. The best public building in most towns is the hospital, while the building most in need of repair is the school. Our highest-paid professionals are physicians, while our lowest-paid professionals are teachers. We have too many hospital beds and not enough schoolrooms.

## 6. Ethical Demands

We have confused positive rights with negative rights. According to Robert Blank, "What began in the writings of John Stuart Mill and Immanuel Kant as a negative right of noninterference has commonly come to be thought of as a positive entitlement— the right to have whatever we want, especially if someone else is paying for it." Thus, we have felt that we have a duty to sustain a patient in a permanent vegetative state, even if the ethical demands of that duty prevent us from providing meals on wheels, or emergency response systems, or respite care, or dental services for the group. Similarly, our medical and legal cultures allow a mother to demand that the taxpayers subsidize an anencephalic infant even though substantial medical needs are going unmet blocks away.

The overemphasis on the individual has caused us to lose our perspective and sense of proportion. Public policy has abdicated its duty to weigh and balance all social needs. We tolerate being the only country in the developed world without universal healthcare. We fund too much marginal medicine and fail to fund enough basic healthcare. We spend too much on high-technology medicine and not enough on prevention. America does not look objectively at its entire system, and we pay a heavy price for not doing so.

Health providers often point out that many of the flaws and inadequacies in the healthcare system are beyond their control. They are not responsible for Americans being the most overweight people on earth or the large number of guns loose in America. They didn't cause our national addiction to illicit drugs or tobacco. True, but not the whole story, as Fuchs notes, for if improvement in health is an important goal, and if physicians concede that they are not effective in modifying diet, exercise, drinking, and smoking, and that they are incapable of changing the physical and psychosocial environments that affect health, some reallocation of resources to research and services that have more impact on health may be in order.[5]

American health policy lacks goals, priorities, and a broad moral vision. America has quietly and almost unknowingly backed into spending one dollar of every six dollars of its GDP on healthcare without asking where we are going and how we are going to get there.

**FIGURE 12.** HEALTHCARE SPENDING AS % GDP

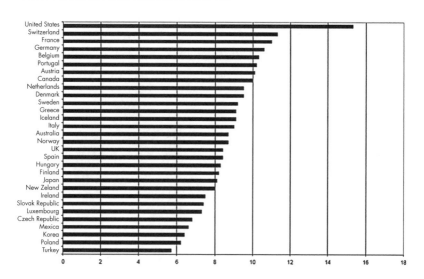

**Note: For countries not reporting 2006 data, data from previous years is substituted.**

*Source:* **Organization for Economic Coordination and Development, OECD Health Data, 2008**

# The Public Advocate versus the Patient Advocate

MEDICINE IS A PROFESSION, HEALTH POLICY A MATTER OF PUBLIC CHOICE AND DEBATE. Both are important, but the macroallocation of health by public policy is vastly different from the microallocation of medicine to patients. The public policy of the health of a nation cannot and should not be judged solely by the quality of its medicine or driven simply by the ethics and culture of medicine. Medicine is a key part—but only a part—of a healthcare system. Doctors' viewpoints are essential but not determinative in advancing a nation's health and structuring its healthcare system. I would suggest that public policy has not done enough to assert the broader public interest in achieving a healthy nation. This has been due to a failure to better distinguish between good medicine and a good healthcare system and the assumption that a good healthcare system makes a healthy nation.

The public policy of health includes medicine, but much more than medicine. Consider the difference in the perspective, standards, and tools available to public policy as opposed to those of a health provider.

| Public Policy | Health Provider |
|---|---|
| Macroallocation | Microallocation |
| Asks: How do you keep a society healthy? | Asks: How do you keep a patient healthy? |
| Tools: Health policy, education, public safety, smoking control, system reform, etc. | Tools: Medicine and teaching health habits |
| Standards: Equal protection, due process, political pressures | Standards: Delivery based on "beneficial" or "reasonable and necessary" |
| Maximize good. | Do no harm. |
| Asks: How does it best deliver health to the society? | Asks: Is it good medicine? |

| | |
|---|---|
| Costs must always be a consideration. | Costs not a consideration (until ten years ago) |
| Maximize health of the group | Maximize health of the patient |
| Asks: Why do people die before their time? Smoking, alcohol, diet, etc. | Asks: What do people die of? Heart disease, cancer, etc. |

The genius of medicine is its devotion to the patient; the duty of public policy is to maximize public goals with limited funds. Public policy builds systems around equal protection, which requires that no citizen be individually advantaged. Public policy must deal with citizens panoramically and must set budgets and priorities. Public policy can never accomplish its goals by leaving the major resource decisions to the health providers. It must make its own independent determination on how it keeps the state or nation healthy. How do we deal, asks Haavi Morreim, professor of philosophy at the University of Tennessee Medical School, with a clash of cultures "in which one side regards economics as irrelevant, while the other considers the ignoring of economics to be irresponsible?"

A patient advocate/public advocate differentiation is inevitable. This is a conflict we have long avoided in the United States, but it must be resolved. Public policy must decide how many public resources it allocates to health and how much of that allocation should go to healthcare, then set some procedures to maximize those healthcare dollars. America is late in joining this ongoing dialogue:

> Making choices about the allocation of resources among competing demands has always existed in European healthcare systems. What is new is the pressure to move from implicit choices made by individual physicians to explicit choices made by a public political process. In recent years several countries including Finland, Netherlands, Norway, Spain and Sweden have established official inquiries to examine priority setting more systematically. . . . There is, however, growing recognition that priority setting cannot be reduced to a technical exercise and that it should be combined with public debate.[6]

Doctors are in a position to judge the quality of a nation's medicine, but it doesn't follow that they are in the best position to judge the merits of the entire healthcare system. Judging the quality of a healthcare system is not a medical judgment but a broader public policy question. Brilliant parts do not automatically make a brilliant system. It is entirely possible for a nation to have brilliant medicine but a poor or inadequate healthcare system.

## A Clash of Cultures

There is, thus, a clash of cultures between medicine and health policy. Health providers are committed to delivering healthcare to their patients, while government's role is to maximize the health of the population generally and in the United States to buy healthcare for specific categories of citizens. The United States has never wanted or seriously considered a government-run healthcare system that has an obligation for the healthcare of all citizens. We have decided to fund most Americans over the age of 65 through Medicare and some of the medically indigent through Medicaid. We have initiated selective other programs such as public health and a program for those with end-stage renal disease. Even in those nations with a universal healthcare system, government looks at its role through very different eyes from those of a health provider.

We must recognize and debate the difference in roles between government and health providers. Health providers look at individual patients; government looks at broad categories of needs of citizens. The focus of the health provider is the patient; the focus of government is supplying multiple services to a broad range of citizens. The language of health providers is to provide "reasonable and necessary" and "beneficial" care for patients; the language of government is a trade-off between multiple priorities.

No government can fund any public good to the level that medical ethics and culture now expect of physicians and patients. Thus, physicians are often ethically required to deliver more medical care than public policy makers can reasonably afford. No public program can meet all individual needs; the model is unsustainable. Health economist Burton Weisbrod asks us to imagine that we have an educational system that pays for everything beneficial for every student, no matter how marginal, and gives the teacher the power to decide what is beneficial. That same teacher has an ethical duty not to take cost into consideration, and the teacher's decisions are automatically funded by government or insurers. Government cannot sustain such a standard even for an important service such as healthcare. We must resolve this clash of medical ethics and culture with the world of public policy and totality of public needs.

One thoughtful observer has described this conflict this way:

> Professionals tend to believe that they are the only ones able to make informed choices. In fact, many of them are not trained to see the overall health situation of the whole population, but only the problems of the individual patients. The devotion of the physician to his/her patient may make it difficult for him not to seek an excessive share of available resources for them and to overlook the resulting loss to other patients.[7]

Physicians understandably have difficulty looking at the social context of disease. Physicians can say yes to one patient without saying no to another. In public policy, everything we do prevents us from doing something else. Paying for treatment A for patient B prevents us from delivering treatment Y to patient Z.

Physicians usually succeed in keeping an individual healthy, whereas government never succeeds in keeping everyone healthy. There are always another thousand sick people, some of them terminal; always an endless need for services. For government, healthcare is Sisyphean. We are saved from one disease to fall into the arms of another disease. We substitute one form of morbidity for another, one form of mortality for another form of mortality. *Cured* is both a medical and public policy victory, but to public policy, it also means live to die later of something else. Robert Blank points out that public policy must ask what no patient advocate can ever be comfortable asking, "Is the price of individual life . . . too high a price for the life and health of society at large?"

Government cannot fund any public service to the satisfaction of the public constituency for that service; it must maximize good within limited resources. Like the old woman who lived in a shoe, government has so many things to do it does not know what all to do. Americans, as citizens, will inevitably demand more services of government than they are willing to fund as taxpayers. Doctors, on the other hand, feel "there is always one more thing that might be done—another consultation, a new drug, a different treatment."

It is, thus, unreasonable and impossible to assume that government policy's goal would be the sum total of the needs of all individual patients. The result of this has been, in the words of George Annas, "doing more and more to fewer and fewer people at higher and higher cost for less and less benefit." Government cannot and should not automatically pay for everything physicians and patients think they need. The government cannot subcontract or delegate to health providers its obligations to weigh and balance all social needs. It is not that we have not been warned. The Oregon Health Decisions group said with brutal honesty nearly two decades ago:

> We cannot live under the idea that we can give everybody all the healthcare they need. Rationing of healthcare is inevitable because society cannot or will not pay for all of the services that modern medicine can provide. People in this state must search their hearts and pocketbooks and decide what level of healthcare can be guaranteed to the poor, the unemployed, the elderly, and others who depend on publicly funded health services.

We have been ignoring the inevitable and delaying the unpopular. John Kitzhaber, first as president of the Oregon Senate and then as governor of Oregon, has been trying to get our attention:

> When money is spent on one set of services, it is, by definition, not available to spend on other services. Healthcare services must compete with all other legitimate services state

government must provide. An explicit decision to allocate money for one set of services means that an implicit decision has also been made not to spend money on other services. That, in essence, constitutes the rationing of healthcare.

So the primary duty of public policy is to maximize total social well-being while the primary duty of the physician is to the health and well-being of the patient. Presently, a physician can often tap the public purse for some marginal need that is beneficial to the patient but diminishes in a society of many needs. Such a power given to physicians to unilaterally spend public money without balancing other social needs is unsustainable, especially where the courts "consider a physician's decision to use a treatment to be de facto evidence of necessity." That's giving the keys to the treasury to the medical profession. It abrogates the public duty to wisely spend resources and leads to decision-making counterproductive to public health. As one frustrated physician said, "If providing Baby K (an anencephalic infant) with prolonged life-sustaining treatment falls within the professional standard of medical care, what possible exception can the physician claim as the basis for withholding any conceivable treatment short of death itself?"

If we can't say no to a baby born without a brain, to whom can we say no? As was well stated by another physician, "If physicians cannot set standards for treatment of anencephalic infants, and adhere to them, standard setting by physicians is a dead issue."

No society distributes public goods in the same way it distributes private goods. The goal of government is to promote the general good. An individual thinking about public safety has different goals and means from public policy makers. Individuals think of burglar alarms, seat belts, locks on doors, and lights in the backyard; government thinks of police departments, courts, and prisons. Individuals dig wells for water; government constructs water and sewage systems. Individuals think about what cars to buy; government thinks of what roads to build and how to sign them. Simply put, government cannot make public policy an individual at a time.

At the same time, the government has available a wide variety of health strategies other than medicine. The tools of physicians to deliver healthcare include the caring tradition, the learning, and the technology of healthcare. The tools of government to deliver healthcare include socioeconomic conditions, education, housing, jobs, and water quality, in addition to allopathic medicine. Both the focus and the tools available to government vary considerably from those of health providers. America would be healthier if we better understood and debated how these cultures differ.

## What If It Were Your Mother?

LET ME ANSWER FOR MYSELF, UP FRONT, ONE OF THE MOST COMMONLY ASKED QUESTIONS in healthcare: What healthcare would you deny if it were your mother? My answer is the universal answer: Deny her nothing; I want her to have everything! Of course, we all would do everything to save a loved one.

But you cannot build a healthcare system, or any public system, a mother at a time. This is an unfair and unrealistic standard for public policy. I would also want to locate a police station near my mother's home, and I would wish to double her Social Security check, and I would want a floodlight in her backyard and an emergency response system in her every room. And I would hope not to pay for any of it. But applied to all our mothers, that road leads to national bankruptcy. The mother test is a good yardstick for your own money but is not a sustainable yardstick for a health plan, however heartfelt.

Every health plan must look dispassionately and intelligently at what is and what is not to be funded. They must set rules and parameters that apply to all their members equally; mothers cannot be exempted. If some medical procedure is futile or inappropriate or has only a slight chance of succeeding, those procedures can legally and morally be excluded from coverage for all the membership. We can neither give mothers a different standard of care, nor can we bring up the standard of care for all subscribers to the what-if-it-were-your-mother standard.

We are all free to provide our mothers extra safety, income, housing, and clothing, but we cannot use either a health plan or government money to do so. When we pool funds, as we do with taxpayer monies or health premiums, we have to set and live by rational distributional roles. No commonly collected pool of funds (taxes or premiums) can maximize all beneficial care to all stakeholders. This is a reality that must be understood by both citizens and doctors.

American doctors were trained in a culture that maximizes everything in healthcare. As Hafdan Mahler, former head of the World Health Organization, noted, "Everywhere, it appears, health workers consider that the 'best' healthcare is one where everything known to medicine is applied to every individual by the highest trained medical scientist in the most specialized institutions."

It goes without saying that this is an unsustainable yardstick. The price of doing something with commonly collected funds is always that we cannot do everything. The price of joint action is the need to set limits.

Both Medicare and health plans owe a duty to their policyholders, including our mothers, but not only to our mothers. We cannot pay limited premiums and limited taxes and receive unlimited care. We cannot make our fondest hopes and dreams the common denominator for demands on common resources. We are entitled to our equitable share and no more. The good news about modern healthcare is that we can expect a lot. The bad news is that we cannot expect everything.

A wise person once told me, "Maturity is a recognition of our limitations." A mature nation must recognize that no health plan and no nation can meet the mother test.

## From a Physician's Viewpoint

THE DOCTOR-PATIENT PERSPECTIVE IS THE MOST IMPORTANT PERSPECTIVE IN HEALTHCARE. It is a healing perspective, concentrating on the patient, focusing modern skills in a two-thousand-year-old tradition that makes the doctor advocate a fiduciary, healer, and confidant of the patient. It is the foundation of healthcare worldwide. This viewpoint lies at the heart of American medicine.

But it is not the only relevant perspective. Expensive modern technology has brought other players to the table. Haavi Morreim points out that these players are not intruders but partners in the health transaction. She explains that doctors serve their patients by spending other people's money and that doctors can only give to their patients what is theirs to give—skills, caring, professionalism, and competence. Someone must separate the nice from the necessary, the clinically possible from the statistically probable. The culture of health providers doesn't allow them to easily take cost into consideration. The culture of public policy demands that cost be a major consideration. No pool of resources can be raised from cost-conscious buyers and spent by health-conscious patients and their passionate advocates without limits. If we didn't have parsimonious third-party payers, we would have to invent them.

For physicians, this appears as distorted as a Dali painting. They vaguely recognize the landscape, but it is contorted, absurd, disjointed, sterile, and surreal. It is devoid of the basic essence of the physician-patient bond.

But modern medicine, for all its genius, makes a new perspective inevitable. Modern medicine has outgrown its metaphors. It is no longer possible for a physician to do everything beneficial for every patient, and clearly cost should be a consideration. Everything a third-party payer does prevents it from doing something else.

The price of modern medicine is the painful necessity to determine limits, make trade-offs, and set priorities. There are endless treatments and procedures that are beneficial to my aging body, endless medical tests that "add value" and relieve my anxiety. In the long run, this cannot be sustainable.

It is true that managed care is starting to change this, but professional standards and public expectations linger on. Much of the recent controversy about healthcare has to do with our refusal to admit that we will have to set limits and make priorities. The ethics of a limited budget are quite different from the ethics developed under an open-ended healthcare system. Once we honestly admit that healthcare is not an open-ended system, the whole dialogue changes. As David Eddy has said,

> The acid test for whether financial resources are limited is to simply ask those who are responsible for budgets of health plans whether they have enough money to do everything everyone wants to do. If not then the budget is limited. We will need to accept, once and for all, that resources are limited. It is the limitation on resources that both necessitates and justifies the strategy of getting more for less.

Ultimately, the health economy must live within the total economy and compete with other social priorities. While we know in our own minds that a nation cannot live by healthcare alone, there is something so compelling about the history of medicine that we tend to think we can explore the entire medical cosmos. Providers do not realize how many alternate uses there are for the money they freely spend. They will take whatever we can give and always ask for more.

A thoughtful book, *Pricing Life* by Dr. Peter A. Ubel, makes an important argument. After dismissing the various arguments on how modern medicine can avoid rationing, Ubel says that a consensus has now developed that some form of rationing is inevitable. Once we face up to the reality of making unlimited demands fit into limited resources, Ubel states, "healthcare rationing will succeed only if physicians relax their advocacy duties occasionally (cautiously and carefully) to ration at the bedside."

He argues that if someone has to set limits, better to have the physician involved in the process rather than excluded. After all, if we have to set limits and draw lines, isn't the physician in a better position to ration than a distant and uncaring insurer? Can't a person's physician better balance the patient's interests with the interests of others covered by the same plan?

Haavi Morreim makes a similar argument. She points out that given all the interventions modern medicine can bring to an aging population, healthcare is simply going to learn to live, every day and every way, with fiscal scarcity. Unlike past rationing, which was rare and isolated, these cost-conscious pressures would be ubiquitous and even more morally troubling. "It is one thing to refuse an item because there is none of it available, and quite another to say that even though it is available, it will not be used because of its expense." But making a virtue out of necessity, she states, "Fiscal scarcity . . . requires us to examine more carefully the legitimate competing claims of society, of payers, of other patients, and of other providers for the healthcare system's limited resources."

Dr. Howard Hiatt makes a related point in his well-known article "Protecting the Medical Commons" when he argues that physicians must play an integral part in determining the rationing polices and priorities, for, however burdensome, no other entity can begin to do it as well. A physician cannot stand back and have others make these decisions, or he will essentially lose his clinical authority.

Public policy makers can never correctly judge medical procedures or technology until we learn to set priorities within medicine and, additionally, have some way of weighing our health considerations with other social demands. In a world of limited resources, public policy must inevitably suboptimize the publicly funded healthcare delivered to the individual so that we can maximize the health of the group or society. So also must health plans. These words sound harsh to the American ear, but no society can afford all the benefits of any social good that it would like or that it would consider beneficial. Pretending this is not so has a larger price than most of us admit. By not coming to grips with the questions of trade-offs and limits, we continue to move untold resources into marginal medicine while other important social needs are going unfilled. Our medical school culture, our legal system, and our third-party reimbursement system all are programmed to deliver more medicine to the patients in a plan than the plan can reasonably pay for.

Important public services such as education, job training, and maintaining infrastructure have the potential of purchasing more health than many of the things that medicine now does at the margin. This has to be corrected if we are ever to maximize health in our society. Hospitals in Colorado (and nationwide) build atriums blocks away from myriad people who are without health insurance. Trucks that deliver new, expensive technology (which is not only duplicative but also only marginally better than what it replaces) pass schools where the teachers have to buy school supplies out of their own pockets. Medical schools are turning out unnecessary physicians and superfluous specialists in a number of cities where the police respond to ringing burglar alarms without bulletproof vests. We have trained more medical specialists than we need, yet many public schools are using outdated textbooks. We blindly subsidize the well-to-do elderly and, at the same time, leave women without prenatal care and more than 40 million Americans uncovered by health insurance. We unnecessarily deny more people healthcare than any other industrialized country. Is this the best healthcare system in the world? It is not.

There is little discussion on how other social or economic measures might buy us far more health for the same money and no discussion that an aging society needs less investigation of the obscure and more investment in the realities of aging (e.g., diabetes, hearing loss, vision, and cognitive memory capacities). We will soon be tempted to spend huge new resources for screening our bodies and genes for risks, some profound and some slight.

Some of our new medical technologies have been developed as if some charitable foundation, for well-meaning reasons, offered to put in a fancy Olympic-size swimming pool and ice-skating rink in the center of the inner city—done without considering what else is going on in that society and with no full weighing of the values and policy considerations involved. Of course, it would be useful and justifiable within the isolation of a question such as, Wouldn't it be beneficial? But it does not consider the core reality of whether that money would buy more recreation, more health, more benefit to the community by some alternative use of the money.

# Needed: A Broader Social Vision

IT HAS BEEN PUBLIC POLICY MALPRACTICE TO FUND OUR HEALTHCARE DELIVERY SYSTEM without better asserting the broader public or societal interest. One cannot and should not build a healthcare system by focusing only on individual needs. Further, it has been a mistake (albeit well-intentioned) to assume that taxpayer or pooled funds should be distributed to health providers to reimburse all treatments they deem necessary based on a medical culture where, until recently, cost is not a consideration. Public policy has too frequently deferred to physicians in building health policy.

Public policy has allowed health providers to be the definers of the health of the nation and the chief architects of its healthcare system. We have allowed health providers to impose their doctor-patient ethics and culture on taxpayer monies without accountability or oversight. Public policy has casually accepted the medical model and allowed doctors to define the scope and demands of that model. But a healthy nation is more than the sum of its physician-patient (or health provider-patient) relationships.

We have been blinded by the brilliance of our medicine, and our public policy reflects this loss of perspective on the total picture. There is a certain moral myopia in a society that spends $1.2 million on a one-in-a-hundred chance to save a set of conjoined twins but fails to provide basic health insurance to millions of others, or in a society that pays for Viagra under a public program but misses 40 million of the medically indigent, mostly working poor. How can a moral society adopt an end-stage renal disease program, the fastest-growing group of users being over 85, before it covers all its women with prenatal care or all its citizens with basic healthcare? How can we keep a woman alive in a persistent vegetative state for more than forty years in Washington, DC, which has the highest infant mortality rate in the nation? Who is or should be looking at the broader public interest? By what standards and yardsticks should we judge public policy success?

It is unreasonable for health policy makers to expect answers to these questions from patient advocates. Patient advocates, of necessity, concentrate on individual trees, not forests. Allowing doctors to focus on the patient and the hospital to focus on who comes through the door allows them to ignore what is going on down the street or across town. That focus allows them the concentration that is so necessary in healing. But in public policy, as in life, our strengths are often our weaknesses. Devotion to their patients makes doctors inadequate judges of the total system. They do a good job for their patients, and this allows health providers to avoid blame for societal shortcomings and to be proud of their professions.

The house of healthcare has always been built around a specific patient and a specific provider. Public policy doesn't have that luxury and must consider the total moral landscape. That landscape has shifted in the last ten years as we have recognized that we simply can't do for everybody everything that medical science has developed. We can no longer tolerate medicine assuming unlimited reimbursement for all beneficial treatments where cost is never a consideration.

You cannot achieve a just and ethical public policy by considering only medical ethics. Macroallocation requires a very different kind of moral calculus. It forces us to develop strategies that maximize the health of the group, and in doing so it occasionally violates medical practices and ethical standards developed in an earlier time under assumptions of unlimited resources.

But now we are being forced to develop new thinking that takes us beyond the traditional boundaries of medical practice and ethics and forces us to consider total social needs. We cannot allow one societal good, healthcare, to dominate and crowd out all other needs of a modern society. Nor can we allow excessive needs of one person in a health plan to deny important care needed by another person in that plan. Preventing this will require a larger and more humanistic social vision than our current dialogue allows.

# Recognizing That Universal Coverage Is a Two-Front War

AMERICA HAS NOT ADEQUATELY CONFRONTED WHAT IS NECESSARY TO ACHIEVE UNIVERSAL access to healthcare. Other industrialized nations have found it relatively easy to achieve universal healthcare because they simultaneously grant all citizens some level of health benefits. Politicians love to give and constituents love to receive additional benefits. The difficulty in covering the uninsured is not in the nature of the benefit, it is that the constituency to be covered is so small that it lacks critical mass to help pass the legislation. Healthcare spending is among the most popular forms of governmental spending. What is difficult is achieving universal coverage in stages. The United States achieved healthcare coverage in stages: healthcare for the employed and their dependents starting in the World War II era, then Medicare and Medicaid coverage starting in 1965. When most people are already covered, it is immensely difficult to get the political consensus to cover those remaining—especially if they lack political power.

This is particularly true in the United States, with its ethic of individualism. We have a less-developed sense of community. Appeals to civic solidarity seem to fall on deaf ears. But we are stuck with our history and have to cope with a situation in which 16 percent of the population has no health insurance and 84 percent are covered under one program or another.

Let us suggest that we will not achieve universal coverage until we develop a new political strategy. America has remained unmoved by the stark fact that people are without coverage. To say, "We are the only nation in the world without universal health coverage" sounds like a brag to part of our citizenry. But there are also some more practical reasons. We have some suggestions that may not be enough but would at least remove some of the barriers.

Achieving universal access is a two-front war. I believe that we must confront directly both conservative thinking and liberal thinking—no easy task. We must persuade people of a conservative mind-set that they have a human obligation to cover all citizens and persuade people of a liberal mind-set that they inevitably must set some limits.

Setting limits goes against the American grain. But it must be done if we are to attain universal coverage. Virtually every healthcare program passed by either state or federal government in the last forty years has ended up costing five to ten times the original cost estimate. Healthcare is among the fastest growing costs for individuals, government, and business. In setting up a universal healthcare system, we must recognize that a modern government has multiple demands and that a healthcare system can be a fiscal black hole into which we could pour literally all of our tax resources. There is no better example of this than the history of Medicare and Medicaid, both of which were dramatically more expensive than original estimates. Universal access demands that we confront the trade-off between quality and quantity, between access and intensity. We can fund a lot but not everything. The price of compassion in a modern healthcare system is restriction.

We must set limits on what we cover in areas such as home healthcare, mental health, alternative medicine, and prescription drugs and decide what we can do about healthcare for illegal aliens. A sophisticated healthcare system is a magnet. In the era of easy transportation, we could have much of the world immigrate, legally or otherwise, to take advantage of our best medicine. We cannot be the healthcare system to the whole world.

We must also challenge the concept that the United States has an exceptional healthcare system. It is hard to get people politically aroused when they continue to hear, unchallenged, that the United States has the best healthcare system in the world. (What could possibly be wrong with the best healthcare system in the world?) That hubris must be addressed headfirst. It is one thing to observe that we have the best medicine or the best-trained doctors. But good medicine is only one part of achieving a good healthcare system. We should not lightly dismiss the World Health Organization's listing the US healthcare system as 37th out of 191 in terms of efficiency.

The bottom line is an expanded moral vision—one that balances who is covered with what is covered. We must look at rationing not only in terms of individuals but also in terms of society.

# Doctors Have Patients, Governors Have Citizens

DESPITE EIGHT YEARS AS A COLORADO LEGISLATOR, I KNEW VERY LITTLE ABOUT HEALTH-care when I was inaugurated as governor in 1975. In those days, a state legislator didn't need to understand much about health policy. The legislature funded Medicaid, but the program ran mostly according to federal regulations. By 1975, healthcare was growing at more than twice the rate of the economy, however, and I felt it could no longer be ignored. A governor is reelected or defeated in good measure by how he manages the state budget; basic self-interest demanded that my administration explore this explosive rise in health costs and identify the options available to expand health coverage to the medically indigent. I was governor of Colorado for twelve years. Today, twenty-five years after leaving the governor's mansion in Denver, access to the system and the challenge of controlling costs of healthcare remain my major interests.

In the legislature, I had represented a blue-collar district comprising union workers, firefighters, shoe clerks, fast-food workers, and small-business owners—hardworking people with big hearts but small budgets. Families in which both parents worked but often could not afford to go to a movie and those without health insurance coverage through their jobs generally went uncovered. Many lived with the knowledge that they were one health episode away from bankruptcy. They didn't want much from me or from government except that we be honest and careful with their tax money, which at the time was scarce for new programs.

Through the political process, I saw what physicians often don't see, those people who cannot fully access the system: men with hernias, children with correctable birth defects, women without adequate prenatal care. Those million-plus uninsured Coloradans were not mere statistics to those in the neighborhood.

I asked our budget staff if we could reprogram some existing health spending and use it to provide healthcare for the working poor. Their response opened my eyes. They pointed out that Colorado had substantial excess capacity in most of our medical infrastructure. The great contradiction of healthcare in this country is that excessive capacity in our medical infrastructure consumes large resources while hundreds of thousands of state residents go without health insurance. This story is repeated in most states. Healthcare has become a metaphor for America: it is filled with good, loving, dedicated people and awesome technology, but it is awash with excess, inefficiency, and unmet needs. It does too much for some and not enough for many.

## Working at Cross-Purposes

One area where Colorado avoided excess was in the number of schools for health professionals. We had (and have) one excellent health sciences center, which has been the intellectual epicenter for healthcare practice and professional education in Colorado. I thought of it as a necessary ally to make change happen in expanding health coverage for the medically indigent. Turning to the University of Colorado Health Sciences Center for help, I discovered that it, like all the other institutions, saw the excess capacity in the system, but, in its eyes, none of it was at the health sciences center. It had ambitious plans for expansion, as had most other public and private institutions in Colorado. Meanwhile, no one owned the problem of excess capacity or the uninsured. Committed, well-meaning doctors practiced spare-no-cost medicine on those lucky enough to be admitted to the system, while nearby there were half-empty hospitals, underutilized and duplicative medical technology, and more medical specialists than in most cities Denver's size. Physicians focused so much on their specialties that they didn't see the unmet needs around them. They favored universal coverage but were unwilling to give up any of their functions or any of their funding. Nobody owned up to the problem of the medically indigent—not the health sciences center, not the state's practicing physicians, not the hospitals, and not the professional organizations.

When I asked the chancellor of our health sciences center why Colorado taxpayers were helping to train so many specialists who often moved out of state when we needed family practice doctors, he pleaded that they were doing desperately needed research. Was that enough of a reason to train surplus medical specialists when the money could buy more health by covering the medically indigent? The health sciences center was busy pushing up the ceiling of medical possibilities, while I was trying to build a floor under those who had no coverage.

Colorado's doctors would, at the time, repeat that in medicine, "Cost is never a consideration." But healthcare was the fastest-growing segment of my budget, demanding increasing amounts of public funds for the medical school, for new equipment at the hospital, and for Medicaid. Daily, if not hourly, hospitals in my state would casually appropriate state funds for a high-risk, low-benefit procedure. I knew those funds could easily save more lives elsewhere in the healthcare system or outside of it, say, by hiring three new schoolteachers, fixing a broken sewer main, or adding two police officers to a high-crime area for a year. How could cost not be a consideration in making a public budget?

In the tight little universe of patient advocacy and health provider professionalism, healthcare providers were allocating taxpayer funds and insurance funds without regard to any other alternative uses of the money. Taxpayers now fund more than half the costs of US healthcare, yet the legislative process demands no accountability for the money as it would in other areas of government spending.

## A Clash of Two Cultures

THE CLASH OF CULTURES BETWEEN THE PATIENT ADVOCATE AND THE PUBLIC ADVOCATE was never so clear as when, in the late 1970s, Dr. Tom Starzl wanted to expand the transplant program at the University of Colorado Health Sciences Center. Tom Starzl was not only one of Colorado's leading doctors, he was also a leading citizen and a friend. His dedication to and promotion of transplantation illustrates the different moral universes of medicine and public policy. He wanted more staff, more resources, and more emphasis on transplantation. I felt Colorado's next priority should be expanding coverage.

Each of us argued our cases publicly in the journal *Dialysis &* *Transplantation*, but despite our best efforts, the dialogue seemed to be a conversation between the blind and the deaf. Dr. Starzl wrote eloquently about two of his cases, a 13-year-old girl and a 76-year-old woman—both of whom benefited from transplantation. I wrote about all the other unmet medical needs in Colorado. It was unthinkable to me to expand the transplantation program when 600,000 state residents lacked basic health insurance. It was unthinkable for Dr. Starzl to turn down anyone who might benefit from a transplant. When I asked why we had to duplicate transplantation facilities available in other states and suggested that Colorado should cover our medically indigent first, he accused me of being anti-research. I countered that research is wonderful, but I was first in favor of maximizing the health of Coloradans. To Dr. Starzl, I was backing away from a world-class program. In his words, "The failure of Mr. Lamm to take advantage of what has happened under his own sponsorship [i.e., Dr. Starzl's success in my early years as governor] is like giving birth to a beautiful child and then trying to starve it so that it will not threaten the food supply." Neither of us was soft-spoken.

The center of a doctor's moral universe is the patient, and the doctor's role as patient advocate has been an important part of two thousand years of medicine. Dr. Starzl was not about to let anyone die if he could avoid it, no matter what the cost, no matter the other health needs of Colorado. Foreshadowing a dialogue that would explode a decade later with the rise of HMOs, my comments indicated that money could save more people if it were spent elsewhere in the system. I felt a moral responsibility to maximize the dollars that were so painfully plucked from the pockets of my constituents and to weigh all public needs in deciding which unmet needs to address. Dr. Starzl believed that America had the best healthcare system in the world, but I disagreed. Our system was then and is today inadequate because it doesn't permit all Americans access to medical miracles, only those with health insurance coverage or the ability to pay out of pocket for medical services. An educational or highway system would never be considered adequate if it left 14 percent of its citizens without schools or transportation, as is and was the case, with 14 percent of our citizens not having access to Colorado's healthcare system.

## Saying No to Dr. Starzl

DR. STARZL IS A SUPERSTAR, AND I HONOR HIS ACCOMPLISHMENTS, BUT COLORADO needed basic healthcare for its medically indigent before it needed a world-class transplantation program. The two of us were living in different moral universes. It is easy for people to say, "Why not have both?" but making a budget is also the deepest expression of one's values and priorities, and I felt that Colorado taxpayers' next priority should be to expand coverage.

"It was a pity to terminate the discussion," wrote Dr. Starzl. "Mr. Lamm's was a description and defense of statistical morality, and mine was the same justification of the doctor-patient relationship which I had used as my lifetime ethical standard."

Dr. Starzl's final written rejoinder captured perfectly the conflict between medicine and public policy. The health providers' tool kit contains the miracles of modern medicine and pharmacy, but public policy has a wider range of options, including public health, education, smoking cessation, highway safety, and so on. Dr. Starzl is a great doctor because he concentrates on his specialty and applies it with considerable caring to individual patients. But his compassion was trumping other important health needs, such as expanded basic health coverage, those that I felt had a higher priority and could have improved health for more people.

The exchange with Dr. Starzl, both verbal and in the literature, still haunts me. He is absolutely right, according to his culture. But walk awhile in my shoes. In a world where cost is inherent in every decision, how do public policy makers fund the needs and demands of a profession where cost is no consideration or look at public need only through the eyes of their profession? How do we compare healthcare needs with other important social priorities? Dr. Starzl is not alone, of course. The whole American public has come to feel entitled to what no nation can financially deliver—all the healthcare that is or may be beneficial to their health. The dilemma of democracy is that citizens want more services as consumers than they are willing to pay for as taxpayers. The ultimate challenge to an aging, technologically blessed society is to adjust public expectations and medical practice to what the society can realistically afford. No society can afford to have one part of its budget, healthcare, grow at the rate ours has averaged for the last thirty years.

Public policy cannot be evaluated or controlled by medical ethics developed by even as dedicated a doctor as Tom Starzl, not when doing so prevents us from serving the broader healthcare and other needs of the taxpaying public. We must better address this clash of cultures.

A decade later, Governor John Kitzhaber, a brilliant political leader and doctor, with the support of the Oregon Medical Society, passed the Oregon Prioritization Plan, which maximized coverage of the medically indigent and paid for it by denying some high-cost/low-benefit procedures such as transplants.

The house of health ethics and policy has more than one floor. The first floor and the most important floor is the doctor-patient relationship, but it is not the only floor. Health plans are also fiduciaries of the funds they collect, and, likewise, the state is a fiduciary of the funds collected from taxpayers. These fiduciaries also have their own moral duties, and those are not exactly coterminous with the historic doctor-patient relationship. The state's ethical options go beyond funding this relationship. In exercising the state's fiduciary relationship, we cannot be judged solely by that doctor-patient relationship.

## A Tale of Two Governors

THE 1995 INTERVENTION OF THEN VIRGINIA GOVERNOR JAMES GILMORE IN THE CASE of a patient in a permanent vegetative state raises important issues of the role of a state in healthcare and insight into how different governors and states view the state's role and obligation for the health of their citizens.

Governor Gilmore attempted to intervene to force Michele Finn, as the legal guardian of her husband, Hugh Finn, to replace her husband's feeding tube after she had ordered it discontinued. Finn, a television newscaster, had spent three and a half years in a persistent vegetative state following an auto accident. His wife asserted that, as legal guardian, she was merely carrying out the wishes of her husband not to live in such a condition, and under Virginia law, food and water may be withheld from people diagnosed in a persistent vegetative state. The governor disagreed and somehow saw it to be his role to intervene in this family tragedy.

Three different courts, including the Virginia Supreme Court, turned down the governor's petition, refusing to second-guess Michele Finn. The Virginia Supreme Court found that withholding nutrition from a person in a permanent vegetative state only allows the natural process of dying and is not a mercy killing.

Contrast the Virginia case with that of Oregon's Medicaid law. As a practicing physician and (at that time) senate president, John Kitzhaber led the fight to not pay for transplants under Oregon's Medicaid law but instead to use the resources to maximize the number of medically indigent citizens who were covered under Medicaid. Identified people were denied solid organ transplants amidst national publicity. Kitzhaber stressed that the state's obligation was to decide both who was covered and what the level of benefits would be. These two cases raise the issue of the depth and breadth of the state's obligation to its citizens and how that obligation contrasts with the obligations of a physician.

This is not an idle question. Medicaid has been, since its inception in 1965, one of the largest and fastest-growing parts of state budgets. The state government is the largest purchaser of healthcare in every state. The programs appear in a variety of places in each state budget, but cumulatively they represent a significant part of every state budget: Medicaid alone is now more than 20 percent of the average state budget, but states additionally fund health insurance for state employees, uncompensated care, the mental health system, the prison system, workers' compensation, and so forth.

Most state policy makers never add up these items because they appear not only in a variety of budget lines but under the jurisdiction of different committees. They are often obscure budget items found under Benefits or in such places as the corrections (inmate health) or higher education (e.g., medical schools) budgets.

Taxpayer monies, state and federal, now pay for approximately 50 percent of the nation's healthcare. Hugh Finn was on Medicaid and was thus funded with both federal and state taxpayer funds. What is the policy and ethical context to evaluate the contrasting actions of these two governors?

What health needs should a state pay for its citizens and what should it not pay for, and by what system does it decide? How do we judge the compassion and justice of a state's health programs? What is the moral radius of a state's interest and concern? By what yardstick do we compare whether Governor Gilmore or Governor Kitzhaber better served the public interest?

We might first ask how Governor Kitzhaber's role compares to the role of Dr. Kitzhaber. Governor Kitzhaber must have a broader role than Dr. Kitzhaber. A governor's patient is the total state. A Governor Kitzhaber macroallocates, while a Dr. Kitzhaber microallocates. A physician is a patient advocate, but a governor, who is the advocate of the entire state, must look panoramically at the whole of the state and maximize good with limited resources. Cost must be a consideration in virtually every public policy decision. Uninsured citizens may concern a physician, but they are not in the same moral radius as they are with a governor.

Dr. Kitzhaber can concentrate fully on making a patient well. Governor Kitzhaber lives in a world of trade-offs and priorities. Governor Kitzhaber not only has the power to make his patients physically well, but he also knows in doing so he has the power to make his state economically sick. A state budget contains many important public needs. Every time a governor says yes to one public need, he or she is indirectly saying no to another.

Governor Kitzhaber cannot focus on his citizens one at a time, and he must differentiate between health policy and medical practice. He cannot blindly fund healthcare any more than he can blindly fund schools, roads, prisons, and so on. To govern is to prioritize, choose among trade-offs, and decide who gets what. It is not a do-no-harm world. A governor is awash in a sea of important and conflicting demands. Public needs cannot be the cumulative total of all individual needs. In public policy, one part of the system is maximized at the expense of other parts of the system.

Governor Gilmore was concerned that Hugh Finn be treated fairly and compassionately but did not indicate in any way that this was part of a larger question of maximizing good with limited resources. If he considered the opportunity costs of that spending, he did not articulate them. Governor Kitzhaber openly struggled with his compassion as a doctor and his obligation as a public policy maker. Recognizing that a state couldn't pay for everything for everybody, he reasoned:

> We must devise a system to allocate our limited resources in a way that is guided not by emotion, but by conscious social policy built on sound ethical and clinical principles and which forces both public policy makers and human-service advocates to assume responsibility and accountability for their actions. The solution means shifting the focus of the debate from an individual to a societal level. Instead of debating which individual should receive a given service and which should be denied, we should instead be debating the funding priority assigned to each specific service.

We must assume that both governors were following their convictions and values. The social impact of the Medicaid system in these two states varies considerably. In 1996, if a family of three made more than $2,880 in Virginia, they were ineligible for Medicaid, while in Oregon a family of three could earn $12,980 before losing their Medicaid. Thus, Virginia would pay for healthcare for this family only if they earned less than 22 percent of the federal poverty level, while Oregon would cover this family if they earned up to 100 percent of the poverty level. The average nationwide rate is 40 percent.

No state policy maker could, in good conscience, sign the Hippocratic oath. The public policy process is to maximize good, knowing that always many needs (i.e., avoidable harm) are going unmet. Finding it impossible to do no harm, public policy makers try to maximize good. It would seem that from a public policy standpoint, Governor Kitzhaber and Oregon came closer to maximizing good than Governor Gilmore and Virginia. From a public policy viewpoint, just because all physicians treat their patients ethically doesn't mean the state has an ethical system.

John Kitzhaber, balancing his viewpoint both as a physician and as a state senator, clearly felt there was a moral difference between a physician's obligation to a patient and the broader obligations of public policy. In a world of trade-offs, can we honestly say that the dollars spent at the end of life are morally superior to the dollars spent (or not spent) on the medically indigent in the prime of life?

One of the basic dilemmas of modern health policy is that when a plan develops strategies that maximize the health of the group, it often violates ethical standards developed in an earlier time around individuals. Once a state decides to cover some part of its low-income population, it has to decide a multilateral equation: what services to provide to which low-income individuals.

It would seem to me that the question isn't whether the Oregon prioritization process is ethical but whether it is ethical not to have such a system. Whenever infinite demands meet limited resources, priorities must be set. A state, faced with multiple public demands and needs, must also prioritize among the total needs. Should not its legislators consider what no physician would ethically consider, i.e., the impact of health spending on other social priorities?

Virginia and Oregon are two examples of the catch-22 that American public policy inhabits. Public policy is driven by ethical standards and culture that are bound to bankrupt both state and federal budgets, while at the same time it allows us to ignore larger, more important nonmedical funding for other social needs. It allows us, indeed encourages us, to ignore the big picture. We fail to ask, With all this talk about medical ethics one individual at a time, do we have an ethical system?

No profession is an island unconnected from the mainland of the economy. From a public policy viewpoint, we have built the house of medical ethics on an inadequate foundation. To the extent that tax-payer monies fund our healthcare system, that system must prove its worth amidst competing social needs. Our moral standards must be consistent with our fiscal realities and the survival of our other social priorities. The ethics of good intentions must be grounded in economic reality. Governments simply cannot write into law, nor can they base a reimbursement system, on a code of ethics developed by a profession. This sounds harsh, but isn't it necessary if we really are going to take seriously the World Health Organization's comprehensive definition of health (complete physical, mental, and social well-being)? If public policy allows healthcare ethics to trump all other considerations, we risk having a medical Taj Mahal amidst massive social squalor. Public policy tries to bring social balance to the total society and cannot allow one category of needs in the name of ethics to trump all other social considerations.

## The Failure of Success

TOWARD THE END OF HIS 1998 STATE OF THE UNION SPEECH, PRESIDENT CLINTON issued this challenge in asking for funding for healthcare research: "I ask you to support this initiative so ours will be the generation that finally wins the war against cancer and begins a revolution in our fight against all deadly diseases." A magnificent goal, but it does raise a disturbing question: What are we going to die of, rust? Do we really want to do away with all deadly diseases? Is this how we should be spending our resources?

One of the reasons that healthcare in an aging society is so expensive is that few things in healthcare have actually saved us money. Marshall McLuhan once observed, "Nothing fails like success." It is worth keeping in mind as we plan for our aging society. A good healthcare system actually increases the number of sick people in a society. It decreases mortality, but it increases morbidity. The more successful we are in treating acute disease, the more we must spend treating chronic disease. The faster we run, the farther behind we fall.

Most of our "miracles" of medicine set us up for more expensive healthcare down the line. Eileen Crimmins makes an important point:

> As mortality declines, those saved from death do not tend to be persons of average constitution but a weaker and frailer group who would have perished under a more severe mortality regime. Thus, with more mortality declines the population becomes more heavily weighted with a frailer group more susceptible to a whole host of diseases and conditions than the average survivor in the population.[8]

In other words, good medicine keeps sick and frail people alive, thereby increasing the number and proportion of sick and frail people in the population.

Some studies show that lifetime healthcare costs of smokers are less than the lifetime healthcare costs of nonsmokers. In any given year, we spend more on healthcare for smokers because it is a terrible, health-impairing habit. Yet, from a systems standpoint, smokers die efficiently. Smokers, on average, die eight years before nonsmokers. Smokers generally die of their first or second disease, while the rest of us have four or five serious illnesses before we die a negotiated death in a hospital or nursing home. The same results follow many of our "cures." We have substantially reduced acute disease to throw ourselves into the arms of chronic disease. There is no cure for old age. Our medical miracles too often become our fiscal failures.

As Henry J. Aaron and Charles L. Schultz observe:

> Improvements in health habits are highly desirable, but not because they would lower costs. Estimates of the economic consequences of a cessation of smoking, for example, indicate that it would generate small net medical savings at best, and would on balance impose overall social costs. Those spared premature deaths from smoking-induced cancers, heart disease, or other sicknesses would eventually die from other more costly illnesses. Alzheimer's disease, for example, would

generate costs even larger on average than those associated with deaths from smoking-induced illnesses.[9]

This does not mean we should stop fighting cigarettes. Cigarettes steal health and cause more than 400,000 US deaths each year. That is the equivalent to the death toll of eight Vietnams every year. We need a smoke-free America because it will make us more healthy and productive—but it will not, in the long run, save us money. Those 400,000 people still die having consumed far more healthcare, nursing home care, and Social Security. Dr. Kip Viscusi, a researcher at Duke, found that smokers actually subsidize nonsmokers by dying before collecting their share of retirement and health benefits. We don't want this to be true, but the evidence seems overwhelming. When all costs are taken into account, smoking saves the government money.

Similarly, many people mistakenly believe that technology will help us avoid some of these hard choices. This appears to be a mistaken hope. Technology enhances the things we can do to aging bodies, but it seldom saves us money. As scholar Sam Cordes observes:

> In most industries, technological innovations are welcomed without question because they generally lead to a less expensive or more efficient production process. . . . However, most technological innovations in the health service industry have added to rather than reduced costs. . . . The question is not whether recent technological developments have added to healthcare costs—they have. The real question is whether the benefits exceed the costs, and in at least some instances they may not.[10]

Neonatology miraculously saves 500-gram babies, but it also gives us yearly a significant new number of disabled. We save people from heart attacks at 75 to have them die of Alzheimer's disease at 85. Because we all must die of something, almost every success ends up costing us more healthcare dollars (and usually more Social Security dollars).

There will always be ten leading causes of death. Sulfa drugs caused a steep decline in the death rate from pneumonia, but preventing fatalities from pneumonia has had the effect of increasing the average duration and expense of other illnesses: senile brain disease, arteriosclerosis, hypertension, diabetes, and similar diseases of aging. So also with preventive care: cost-effectiveness studies, which estimate the net costs and net health benefits of interventions, show that preventive care usually increases medical expenditures.

The Population Reference Bureau published a 1984 study, *Death and Taxes*, which found that curing cancer and curing heart disease would increase federal spending. The authors were not arguing that we should not try, but they wanted us to do it fully realizing the consequences. They found that "the postponement of death increases federal costs, requiring more taxes." Like Faust, we were not fully aware of the trade-offs.

Yes, we should continue to cure disease, but we cannot cure death. Chronic disease at the end of life is far more expensive than acute disease in midlife. An aging society needs a deeper dialogue on how we set limits. Not setting some limits on high-cost/low-benefit procedures will surely waste limited funds and negatively affect our children.

An aging, inventive society, which is already borrowing heavily from our children to fund government and whose economy faces massive international competition, must start a dialogue on how it allocates its scarce financial resources. A society that in the last thirty years has doubled the healthcare share of its GNP must start to realistically look at its options for stabilizing those growth trends. We do not have the luxury of merely tinkering at the margins.

## Better Healthcare through Rationing

CHARLIE BROWN, IN THE COMIC STRIP *PEANUTS*, ONCE SAID, "THERE IS NO ISSUE TOO big that you can't run away from it." This clearly has been the story of healthcare rationing in the United States and in most other developed societies. Certain issues in public policy are much easier to ignore than to confront. If rationing is openly discussed, it will involve specifically denying something, taking away some measure of healthcare that would be beneficial to a particular person. Politicians are not the only people who avoid unpleasant subjects. The healthcare community also ignores and avoids with equal vigor the reality of rationing. Healthcare providers were trained to serve—not deny.

When we are strictly honest with ourselves, we admit that, as a society, we ration. According to authors Henry Aaron and Charles Schultz, rationing occurs when "not all care expected to be beneficial is provided to all patients." We ration whenever we make choices among the claims of individuals who are competing for scarce resources. Much has been written about the approximately 50 million Americans who are not covered by health insurance and about the other approximately 40 million who have inadequate insurance. This is a form of rationing. We ration by price of healthcare and by geographic distribution of patients. We tell each other that this is indirect rationing, and apparently we find this morally much easier to accept than direct rationing. A sin of omission is easier to live with than a sin of commission. We have enough doctors and hospitals, but we do not have the financial resources to do everything for everybody. Difficult choices will have to be made.

Let me present a more positive case for rationing. It is my passionate belief that we can all have better healthcare through rationing. The United States now has the worst form of rationing—rationing people by leaving them out of the system. A society will not start to maximize its healthcare access and quality until it fully confronts the issues involved in rationing.

It is said that a problem well defined is a problem half solved. Most thoughtful health providers now recognize that the genius of American medicine is having invented more healthcare than we can afford to deliver to everyone. A society that is as inventive and creative as ours, which has limited healthcare means, fools itself when it avoids discussing rationing. In fact, our society would benefit from an honest discussion of rationing.

The status quo in healthcare is unsustainable. French researchers once conducted a study in which they asked how much it would cost to give each citizen all the healthcare that would be beneficial. The answer was five and a half times the French GNP. The fatal flaw in this approach is in the yardstick. No modern society can afford to give to each of its citizens all the healthcare that is beneficial. Medical need is an infinitely expandable concept. We "need" what is available.

Just as the individual family must make choices within a budget, so must our national family make choices about what we can and cannot afford. We cannot keep up with healthcare costs that are growing at two to two and a half times the rate of inflation. It is a reality of public policy that anything that grows at this rate of inflation eventually destroys itself. Geometric growth can never be sustained.

Increasing efficiency and ending waste alone do not solve our problem. Rationing is the price we must pay for our creative success. It is the ugly child of the marriage of our technical ingenuity and our egalitarianism.

Granted, the sick will always consume far more healthcare resources, but we know part of the spending on the 1 percent is because of defensive medicine, inappropriate medicine, inability to say no to hopeless cases, or an overemphasis on a patient's unreasonable request ("Do everything you can, doctor.").

All nations ration—some by price, some by queuing, and some by setting priorities. I believe a nation does not maximize its healthcare until it starts to ask the hard question, How can we prioritize our expenditures to buy the most healthcare for the most people? We should not have to apologize for rationing; we should promote it and advance it. We cannot explore the best way to maximize each dollar unless we have a community dialogue about how we put our health dollars to the highest and best use. It is an inevitable dialogue, and we ought to make a virtue out of necessity.

It is increasingly obvious that the genius of American medicine has outpaced our ability to pay. Oregon's plan is a harbinger of how others may try to resolve this debate. Oregon decided to cover everyone under the federal poverty line with Medicaid and prioritize the healthcare it delivers. This legislation identifies, for instance, that prenatal care for many women is a higher priority than transplants for a few. Whether or not Oregon's legislators have the right answer, we should admire them for asking the difficult questions. These legislators are honestly trying to solve the dilemma.

The dialogue about rationing is long overdue. We have institutionalized too much of our healthcare spending. We have to liberate our minds and ask what policies and strategies will buy the most health for our society.

The more I study healthcare, the more I recognize that only a tenuous connection exists between healthcare spending and health. I sit in intensive care units and see the massive amount of money being spent on hopeless cases, and often I think of children without Head Start programs, women without prenatal care, and infants without adequate food. This is more than liberal compassion. Robert Evans has stated:

> A society that would spend so much on healthcare that it cannot, or will not, spend adequately on other health-enhancing activities may actually be reducing the health of its population through increased health spending.

America needs a national dialogue on how we can best keep our people healthy. It needs to examine what other countries have done to maximize healthcare and resources. It makes no sense to transfer a 90-year-old patient with congestive heart failure from a nursing home to an intensive care unit to die when tens of thousands of American women give birth without having received adequate prenatal care. Much of what we do today in the American healthcare system is futile or marginal. We need to discuss our national healthcare priorities. Rationing is not something to be avoided; it is something to be welcomed.

# The Sometime Cruelty of Compassion

TO PARAPHRASE ECONOMIST KENNETH BOULDING, ONE OF THE BASIC DILEMMAS OF public policy is that all of our policy experience deals with the past, and all our decisions relate to the future. These policy decisions will be exacerbated by the very successes of our past. The incredible bounty of the interaction between a sparsely populated continent filled with abundant resources and an energetic people has masked the need for making hard choices. It has allowed us to fool ourselves into thinking that we can satisfy more desires and expectations than we can realistically afford.

Public policy is too often driven by identified needs and identified individuals to the exclusion of other public goods. One of the great challenges of the twenty-first century will be to learn the wisdom of George Bernard Shaw's aphorism: "The mark of a truly educated man is to be truly moved by statistics." Public policy is burdened by the difficulty of making unidentified lives equal to identified lives. Statistics often represent people, not numbers. But, as a nun once told me, "Statistics are people with the tears washed off."

Professor Alan Wertheimer raises the following provocative question.

> Suppose the following were true: At least some money spent on open heart surgery could be used to prevent heart disease. Reducing the number of open heart surgery operations would mean that some patients in need of such surgery might die, but many more lives would be saved by the preventive approach.[11]

He points out that "all involve choosing between a policy designed to help specific persons and one that seeks to prevent the need for such help. . . . We must often choose between helping identifiable lives and saving statistical lives. These choices are especially difficult because we know who needs the help.

Public policy inevitably has to accept casualties. We do not ban automobiles, guns, or alcohol despite annual loss of life, because we judge their utility to be greater than their cost. It is seldom an equal weighing. Identified lives loom so much larger because they have a human face. Statistical deaths, no less human and no less dead, do not have a face—only a number. Not nearly as visible, but human nevertheless. It is not good public policy to ignore these statistics." As author David Eddy observed:

> The statistical life is one of the fifty lives that will be lost in a year because of a government decision not to pursue a particular mine safety regulation. The identifiable life is the one miner trapped in the collapsed mine. We are held hostage to these identified lives—much like a kidnapper holds his/her victims hostage. It is hard not to give in to a ransom note. What seems cruel in an individual case is often actually the most lifesaving and compassionate for the general society.

Joseph Stalin once said, "One man's death is a tragedy; a million men's deaths is a statistic." In a horrible way, Stalin was right, and his reasoning applies to the American healthcare system. "We don't mind throwing people overboard," says one wag, "we just don't want to hear the splash." In the same spirit, Governor Kitzhaber has said, "Legislatures have never had to confront the victims of silent rationing or be accountable for the very human consequences. It is like high-level bombing where the crew never sees the faces of the people they are killing." George Bernard Shaw had it right; we must be educated and compassionate enough to be moved by statistics.

We do many things at great expense to avoid having to say no to identified lives. The United States has approximately three times the percentage of intensive care beds than other industrialized nations, yet we don't save any more of the critically ill. We have far more specialists than other industrialized countries. We spend billions of dollars to avoid having to make the everyday life-and-death decisions that other countries make routinely. Then we turn around and leave more than 40 million Americans without health insurance.

We spend more billions on expensive neonatology units, often to save preemies that will cost more millions and have little or no quality of life, but we do not give prenatal care to many American women. That is neither good nor compassionate health policy.

## Lessons from Great Britain

ONE OF THE MOST INTERESTING DAYS I SPENT IN THE HEALTHCARE FIELD WAS IN GREAT Britain with a home health worker who visited women who had recently given birth. The home health worker who accompanied us had no formal education, but she had raised a lot of children and grandchildren of her own. Her job was to go around after the birth of children and see that the mothers were recovering and the babies thriving.

Every mother in Great Britain gets all the prenatal care she needs plus three postnatal visits from a home health worker. Great Britain has far fewer neonatology units, but the British ask the key question, How do we maximize the number of healthy mothers and healthy babies? They may not miraculously save 500-gram identified lives, but their maternal mortality and infant death rates are better than ours in the United States, which means their approach saves many more mothers and babies.

We make a movie about the search for the high-technology cure for a little boy named Lorenzo but hardly give a thought to the approximately 70,000 women who gave birth last year without adequate prenatal care.

Governor Jeb Bush of Florida gets international publicity for seeking and signing legislation overriding a husband's decision to terminate nutrition and hydration for his wife who had been in a permanent vegetative state for thirteen years, yet Florida has close to 20 percent of its population without basic health insurance.

British novelist Iris Murdoch wrote, "Seeing is a moral art." She said our "moral quality functions in what we see and remember and know." Before we can correct a problem we have to see the problem and put it in moral perspective.

That we must do in reforming US healthcare. We must have

the moral wisdom to see that while we can do whatever we want with our own money, when we fund healthcare with common funds, we have a moral duty not to unjustly overconsume those funds. We must see that our health plan co-members are real people with real needs of their own.

## What Is a Natural Death?

AUTHOR LYNN PAYER BRILLIANTLY DESCRIBES THE AGGRESSIVE CULTURE OF AMERICAN medicine: "From birth—which is more likely to be by Cesarean than anywhere in Europe—to death in hospitals, from invasive examination to prophylactic surgery, American doctors want to do something, preferably as much as possible."

It is shockingly difficult today for someone in the United States to achieve a natural death. Approximately 80 percent of us die negotiated deaths in either a hospital or a nursing home. Those who are sophisticated enough to follow the rules can refuse medical treatment whether they are competent or incompetent at the time of the decision. A competent adult patient, of course, is legally entitled to refuse medical treatment of any sort for any reason. For the incompetent patients, a number of court cases (Quinlan, Saikewicz, Spring, and Eichner) give precedent that an incompetent patient might act by a proxy exercised by a family member or guardian. All but a few states now have specific legislation for living wills and durable powers of attorney.

How natural is natural death? In her book *Ethics in the Sanctuary*, Margaret Battin weighs in with her interpretation:

> An untreated respiratory death involves conscious air hunger. This means gasping, an increased breathing rate, panicked feeling of inability to get air in or out. Respiratory deaths may take only minutes; on the other hand, they may last for hours. If the patient refuses intravenous fluids, he may become dehydrated. If he refuses surgery for cancer, an organ may rupture. Refusal of treatment does not simply bring about death

in a vacuum, so to speak; death always occurs from some specific cause.

She goes on to observe:

Even less likely to match the patient's conception of natural death are those cases in which the patient is still conscious and competent, but meets a death that is quite different than he had bargained for. Consider the bowel cancer patient with widespread metastases and a very poor prognosis who— perhaps partly out of consideration for the emotional and financial resources of his family—refuses surgery to reduce or bypass the tumor. How, exactly, will he die? This patient is clearly within his legal rights in refusing surgery, but the physician knows what the outcome is very likely to be: obstruction of the intestinal tract will occur, the bowel wall will perforate, the abdomen will become distended, there will be intractable vomiting (perhaps with a fecal character to the emesis), and the tumor will erode into adjacent areas, causing increased pain, hemorrhage, and sepsis. Narcotic sedation and companion drugs may be partially effective in controlling pain, nausea, and vomiting, but this patient will not get the kind of death he thought he had bargained for. Yet, he was willing to shorten his life, to use the single legally protected mechanism—refusal of treatment—to achieve that "natural" death. Small wonder that many physicians are skeptical of the "gains" made by the popular movements supporting the right to die.

These new realities require us to rethink how we make the best of life's end. The world of death and dying has dramatically changed, and we have to create individual and societal answers that reflect those new realities.

Take, for example, the questions of when and whether to use artificial nutrition and hydration. It is almost an atavistic response to provide food and to assume that it is painful to die from malnutrition or dehydration. Yet "it is very common that people near the end of life quit eating, or at least quit eating much, and quit drinking," explains Dr. Joanne Lynn, a geriatrician and senior associate professor at Dartmouth Medical School. "The question becomes whether we should use artificial means to circumvent their stopping eating, and that turns on whether it does them any good."

Well-meaning people often do not recognize that tube feeding can do more harm than good, can torture not treat. But professionals who treat the dying point out that people who stop all food and fluid do not usually experience pain. Dr. Lynn writes:

> It is likely that prolonged dehydration and starvation induce no pain and only limited discomfort from a dry mouth, which can be controlled. For individuals carrying an intolerable burden of illness and disability, or those who have no hope of ever again enjoying meaningful human interaction, the withdrawal of food and fluid may be considered without concern that it will add to the misery.

But our instincts are all the other way. Dr. Lynn states further, "Our instinct is to provide food. Feeding another person is the way of showing that you care about them, and failure to feed is ordinarily a way of showing that you do not care."

Many commentators recognize that modern technology too often gives us not a longer life, but a longer death. Dan Callahan says the first duty of the healthcare system should be to help young people become old people, not mindlessly postpone death. He points out wisely that if public policy could concentrate on avoiding premature death instead of merely death, it would help considerably in reordering our research and healthcare priorities.

A society that has increasing numbers of elderly, an increasing average age of the elderly, fewer young people and workers, lower productivity growth, and increased medical innovation has reason to ask itself some hard questions.

A healthcare system, if we are to someday attempt to provide universal access to healthcare, must set boundaries and limits. And what better place to start than the substantial resources we expend on people for whom there is no happy scenario. Ultimately, we shall have to go even further.

A woman died a few years ago in Washington, DC, who had been in an irreversible coma for more than forty years. Vegetative, comatose, given no reasonable chance of recovery, she was a living corpse kept alive for more than forty years in a city that desperately needs prenatal care and where children, more often than not, do not have all their vaccinations. As we can see from the recent Florida case of PVS patient Terri Schiavo, a governor can get national attention for intervening in what the medical community said was a hopeless case of PVS; yet no one holds the same governor accountable for failing to even try to cover Florida's uninsured. Governors seem to be held to a different standard for sins of commission than they are for sins of omission.

Ultimately, we will have to stop the illusion of unlimited resources and develop an ethic of restraint and the need for trade-offs. We cannot test people for every possible danger, however remote, and we must not deploy certain new drugs and technologies that marginally improve health at great expense. We must develop cost/benefit studies and stop pouring massive resources into long-shot medicine. We must stop thinking of death as optional. Theologian Paul Ramsey noted the agonizing need to "discover the moral limits properly surrounding the efforts to save a life." He said this nearly four decades ago and we have never taken his challenge seriously.

We will clearly have to ask, What are the ends of medicine? What is it we really want out of the healthcare system? The Hastings Center puts it this way:

> Medicine's historic response to infectious disease and acute, self-limiting diseases of short duration does not offer an adequate way of understanding or responding to the personal, social and ethical challenges posed by chronic illness and disability. What is needed, instead, is a different conception of the proper ends of medicine in the face of chronic illness, and beyond that, a better understanding of the human and social meaning of chronic illness.

I believe for a few high-cost procedures we should make age a consideration in the delivery of healthcare. The unthinkable has become the unavoidable. A society owes a greater duty to perform a transplant on a 9-year-old than on a 90-year-old. We may want to spend vast amounts to save young people with their whole lives ahead of them, but not octogenarians. We should spend less on acute care for the elderly and more on social services such as home healthcare, emergency response systems, respite care, and senior citizens centers. It also requires us, as a society, to decide what we can afford and what makes sense with limited funds.

## Overutilization of the Intensive Care Unit

"WHAT CHANCE IS THERE THAT SHE WILL LEAVE THIS UNIT ALIVE?" I WAS DOING GRAND rounds at the teaching hospital at the University of California Medical School, which sits high above the city on one of San Francisco's storied hills. The group of doctors looked annoyed at my question. We were clustered around the bed of Mrs. P in the intensive care unit. Mrs. P, age 91, had been in the intensive care unit for two weeks, kept alive by a tangle of tubes and hoses. The attending physician swallowed her resentment at my question. "Very small, but every once in a while someone survives. Medicine must do everything possible as long as there is a chance she could get better."

America has approximately 67,000 intensive care units, far more than any other country. An intensive care unit is the most expensive medical setting possible, usually staffed by one to one and a half nurses per bed and equipped with hundreds of thousands of dollars of high-technology equipment. These units do save some people previously lost, but they do so at a very high cost. They are, thus, symbolic of both our caring and our priorities.

We put neonates, born to women who did not receive any prenatal care, in expensive intensive care units. As part of our practice of defensive medicine, we put into these expensive beds people who are terminal and people who are not sick enough to really belong there. Once people get into the system, we spend fantastic amounts of money exploring a small chance of survival, but 50 million Americans do not have basic health insurance, and 30 percent of the kids in America have never seen a dentist. We have seemingly unlimited resources for patients in the system but painfully few for citizens outside the system. Our healthcare spending is reactive and reflexive rather than reflective.

Five percent of our patients, many of them terminal, account for more than 49 percent of our medical costs, yet today Medicaid covers only 40 percent of the people living in poverty, and a million American families have one or more members denied healthcare yearly.[12] Almost 60 percent of Medicare's inpatient expenditures are attributed to 12 percent of the recipients, too often for marginal procedures. In one corner of the hospital, we are squeezing a few more days of pain-racked existence out of people for whom there is clearly no happy outcome; yet our infrastructure is deteriorating, our schools are overcrowded, and millions don't have even basic healthcare.

An alarm goes off and the team rushes to resuscitate a man with prostate cancer. But an alarm has also gone off in our economy that we ignore at our peril. We have staggering trade deficits and worrisome rates of individual and corporate debt. Industry after industry has shrunk, disappeared, or moved offshore. We have one of the lowest rates of saving and a staggering trade deficit, yet a group of our brightest men and women are using expensive Japanese machines and large amounts of our limited resources on frail bodies, many of whom everyone concedes will never leave this unit. On this day, four of the twelve people in the unit have "virtually no chance" of leaving the hospital.

The basic dilemma of American medicine is that we have invented more healthcare than we can afford, yet we find it terribly hard to set priorities. We rush to rescue people in intensive care units today who just yesterday were abandoned by the healthcare system. We spend too much money on high-technology care for a few and too little on basic healthcare for the many. We have spent millions keeping hearts beating in cities where infant mortality rates exceed those of many third world countries. We have thus become a victim of our machines. *Can do* has become *must do*. Our system too often preserves life without preserving health.

Healthcare in America is infinitely expandable. We have the finest technological means in the world, but no one is asking, To what end? Every dollar we spend has an opportunity cost, and increasingly we are spending limited dollars on high-technology medicine for a few, while many go without even basic healthcare. But there's another alarm, and we must be off on our mission of "mercy."

## Death: Right or Duty?

TOO OFTEN THE LIMITS OF OUR LANGUAGE ARE THE LIMITS OF OUR THINKING. "If thought corrupts language, language can also corrupt thought," warned George Orwell. How we label something too often controls how we think about it. We get particular concepts in our head, and they are hard to change. They govern how we think and how we act. Disease and death used to be considered God's will, and it took hundreds of years and no small number of martyrs to get that corrected. It was very hard to develop modern medicine when so many factors were thought of as outside of human control. Similarly, the number of children a woman had was thought to be God's will, and that has made the development of contraception controversial to this day. Human control over any part of human destiny is usually vigorously opposed. Change comes slowly. Humankind has the tendency to confuse the familiar with the necessary.

Science finally overcame many such outmoded concepts, however sincerely held. Medicine has developed ever-more inventive and expensive things we can do to the body as it ages and approaches death. Now language limits us in a different way. Today we have so changed the concept of death that we talk about the right to die as if death were an option. *Right to die* is a useful term in some contexts, but it implies death is a matter within our individual control. Too many Americans think themselves entitled to all healthcare technologically possible, no matter how marginal, and will spend unlimited insurance or government money on long-shot attempts to delay death. We have gone from an attitude of superstition to hubris.

This way of thinking has its own trap. Death is not an option. Shakespeare said it so well, "We all owe God a death." Humanity has a hard time putting death in perspective. Over the history of humankind, we have been alternately paralyzed or dismissive about the concept of death; both actions are wrong and cause substantial harm. We are not helpless in the face of death; there are myriad ways we can postpone it. Likewise, death is not an option. Thinking of death as a right to be exercised misappropriates tens of billions of dollars a year. America spends 27 percent of its healthcare dollars on the sickest 1 percent of its population and 55 percent on the sickest 5 percent. This concentration of expenditures is far above spending patterns in all other developed countries. Insulated against the costs and petrified by the results, our culture, which considers death the enemy, spends more and more on less and less.

We do not have a right to die. Humans are mortal. Death is neither a right nor an option. Yet there is a public policy tragedy in our misconception. Money desperately needed elsewhere in society is being spent on marginal and low-benefit medicine throughout the system but particularly on the dying process. No other society would take a 90-year-old with a terminal disease such as cancer out of a nursing home and put him or her into an intensive care unit. My wife and I were recently at the bedside of a 93-year-old man who had two fatal diseases (metastatic cancer of the prostate and end-stage kidney failure), and he had just been brought into the intensive care unit with a serious stroke. Massive resources were being poured into this gentleman, while blocks away people were going without primary care and kids were going without vaccinations.

Ten percent of US hospital beds are ICU beds, while the rest of the developed world uses 3 percent of its hospital beds as ICU beds. What do we get for our extra intensive care beds? Mostly we get expensive deaths. There is no evidence that we save more critically ill people than other societies. We have failed to develop policies that rationally limit the use of intensive care beds to those who truly benefit. An ICU bed was designed for a realistic salvage attempt, not end-stage care.

I would suggest the sum total of all ethical medicine, as now defined and practiced, is unethical health policy. The hubris in thinking that medicine can deliver to an aging society all the beneficial medicine its inventiveness has developed is misplaced.

Proust observed, "The real voyage of discovery lies not in seeking new lands, but in seeing with new eyes." So also must we see with new eyes. Everything we do in healthcare prevents us from doing something else. We live in a new world of trade-offs but without the ethical standards or yardsticks to choose among them.

It is imperative that we question this concept. My generation's bodies are developing ailments and chronic conditions faster than our economy can fund the treatments. We are spending too much money on the last generation at the expense of the next. We have run into the law of diminishing returns. Modern medicine has presented us with a dilemma: our aging bodies can bankrupt our children and grandchildren. Healthcare is important, but it cannot trump every other societal need. We must begin a dialogue by thinking clearly about death and its costs.

## The Corner Place with Governor Lamm

### "Sacrificial Lamm"

THE PASSAGE IN 1967 OF COLORADO'S ABORTION REFORM LAW, THE FIRST IN THE nation and seven years prior to *Roe v. Wade*, was my first foray into the junction of law and medicine. I was elected to the Colorado legislature in 1966 and took my seat in the Forty-sixth General Assembly in January 1967. Young, naive, and idealistic, I looked for a way to make the world a better place.

Dottie and I had spent five months in South America in 1963 on our honeymoon, living close to the land on two dollars a day. We often stayed in primitive conditions and traveled by bus to many remote areas. We learned in our travels that in South America, generally one-quarter of the hospital beds were taken up by women who suffered botched abortions. We had met and talked with some Catholic priests who were handing out birth control to their parishioners despite the church's ban on artificial birth control. It was clearly less sinful than abortion, which they admitted was an epidemic. Dottie, a feminist even then, was particularly and personally outraged. "How can the law force unwilling women to have unwanted children?"

Most of these victims already had large families and were desperate to limit the size of them. They had no alternative but to get illegal abortions, inevitably by someone without medical training and under bare conditions. Birth control in South America was generally illegal. We saw a male-dominated oligarchy, where the same small group of families would send one son to the family business, one to politics, and one to the church to monopolize most of the wealth and political power and to produce policies that would kill or mutilate thousands of women who felt they could not adequately care for an additional child. We saw clearly in South America, and still believe today, that the law can't say whether a woman will have an abortion, just where. Desperate women, following their own consciences, were going to prevent unwanted pregnancies one way or the other.

But I was a freshman legislator from a heavily Catholic district. I hardly could find my way to my desk. The art of passing successful legislation is the practice of marshalling, and in some cases manufacturing, the necessary support for attainable goals. In a representative government, responding as it must to the wishes of the constituents, legislation is by necessity closely tied up with public opinion. Al Smith, one of the world's most practical politicians, stated it thus, "A politician can't be so far ahead of the band he can't hear the music." It can by definition be no other way. No politician who is too far out front of public opinion will survive politically. But I knew little of this at the time. I was shielded from these realities by my naiveté.

In 1967, *abortion* was not a word used in polite company. It was not a word ever heard on the news and was seldom read in the paper. It was truly a taboo subject, so I was amazed that the more legislators I approached, the more cosponsors signed on to the bill. A frequent comment was they felt the time had come to face this subject. To my great surprise and absolute amazement, virtually every legislator we approached not only agreed to put his or her name on the bill but manifested great enthusiasm. When we were finished quietly contacting the various legislators, we had a total of fifty-three cosponsors, more than half in the House of Representatives and slightly less than half in the Senate.

Two years before, Colorado had succeeded in passing, on a second attempt, a law that provided birth control information to indigent women. The birth control law had been passed, signed by the governor, put into operation, and forgotten. Most legislators were aware that in that case the storms of adverse reaction passed without raining retribution. The wonderful woman who was chiefly responsible for its passage, Ruth Steel, came to my support, as did the wise and effective chief sponsor, Senator John Bermingham.

We argued that we were only slightly expanding the categories under which an abortion could be obtained, while at the same time we were tightening the circumstances under which it would be performed. We decided to expand the grounds of legal abortion to include physical health, mental health, rape, incest, and fetal deformity. Two doctors would have to certify that one of those conditions was present.

We decided to approach the news media and seek their endorsement. The news media were, at the time, the single most important factor in molding community opinion with regard to legislation. It was deemed imperative by us to at least negate opposition on the part of the press and, if possible, to seek its specific endorsement of the proposed legislation. For this purpose, a panel was formed consisting of Senator John Bermingham and myself, representing the two political parties, a doctor, and a minister or rabbi, representing their respective viewpoints. This ad hoc group called upon all the major news media in the Denver area and explained to them our bill. The doctor answered any medical questions, any moral issues were taken on by the clergy, and any legislative questions were answered by the two legislators. The effort proved immensely successful and won us enthusiastic support during the legislative battle in the form of three editorials by *The Denver Post*.

The polls showed what our practical experience taught us, that the public was a long way from accepting an absence of all restrictions whatsoever upon a doctor's authority to approve an abortion. Society felt that it still had a role in dictating circumstances under which an abortion was to be performed. It was easy to argue that the moral issues raised by the opponents of this legislation had long been resolved in the United States; that is, under some circumstances any woman may obtain an abortion to protect herself. To those arguments that the new law was taking a life and thus was unconstitutional, we had the easy retort that no one had ever challenged the constitutionality of any of the other states' abortion laws, including Colorado's, and all we were doing was slightly expanding the categories under which an abortion could be obtained while at the same time tightening the circumstances under which it could be performed. When the question was put as merely a weighing of two rights—between the health and welfare of the mother and the potential human personality of the fetus—the public seemed conformable and satisfied. We stuck closely to what our best judgment told us could be accomplished.

All major attempts at amending the bill on the floor of the House were eventually defeated, and the bill was voted out of the House, going to the Senate in substantially the same form as introduced and passed by the committee. The legislative history of the bill in the Senate was substantially the same as in the House. The bill passed, and after the House concurred in a minor amendment, the bill was sent to the governor for his signature. Governor Love signed the legislation, and Colorado became the first state in the nation to liberalize its abortion legislation. A majority of Republicans in both houses and a Republican governor passed a law that kicked off an ideological war within the Republican Party, which still echoes today.

It was a heady accomplishment for a 32-year-old. I got my picture in *Time* magazine and significant other national press. I was named Outstanding Freshman Legislator and got invited to a number of states to testify on the Colorado experience. I was adopted by a number of abortion rights groups, made speeches, and testified to legislatures around the country. I had made a significant number of enemies and a significant number of friends, but more than anything I had learned how to succeed in the legislative process. From this point on, nothing could match the excitement and rewards of public policy. I was hooked.

# The Book Nook with Dr. Sharma

## Framework for Public Policy

OUR NATION HAS WRESTLED WITH ISSUES SURROUNDING HEALTHCARE REFORM FOR nearly a century. President Theodore Roosevelt attempted to enact universal coverage as early as 1912. Presidents Franklin D. Roosevelt and Harry S. Truman also drafted public health insurance programs but failed due to strong opposition. Readers interested in undertaking a preliminary and historical approach to the issues surrounding healthcare reform should start by first examining books by Colin Gordon or Jill Quadagno. In *Dead on Arrival: The Politics of Health Care in Twentieth-Century America*, Colin Gordon examines the political climate surrounding reform with respect to doctors, patients, hospitals, unions, and employers and provides insight into the failures of healthcare reform. *One Nation, Uninsured: Why the US Has No National Health Insurance* by Jill Quadagno is another informative read. This book also traces the history of US health policy, with the main point being that powerful groups have played a key role in defeating healthcare reform.

A final recommended book is *Boomerang: Health Care Reform and the Turn against Government* by Theda Skocpol. This insightful analysis examines President Clinton's healthcare reform proposal during 1993–1994. In terms of Skocpol's recommendations for gaining support for universal coverage, she suggests that the dialogue surrounding healthcare reform needs to involve a diverse group of Americans, emphasize social justice and moral values, and highlight the positive role of government. If we are to improve population health and find effective ways to curtail healthcare costs, the conversation cannot be one-sided—politicians interacting only with other politicians and interest groups. We need to engage (and educate) the larger public. Most certainly, this requires some sort of local community effort and involvement. This is where we need to garner support for town hall meetings and *incentivize* community participation. Public debates, which are often informative and entertaining, can be one mechanism.

We also need to revisit Ben Franklin's thirteen moral virtues. Some Americans, I fear, have lost sight of industry, justice, moderation, resolution, and sincerity. More specifically, I am suggesting we have become complacent and need to inculcate core values that exemplify pride, inclusion, and humility. How can we instill these? This is no easy task—our American ideals and values have been eroding for more than a century. To correct our course, we need political leaders who have a moral compass and believe in public spirit and not self-interest. We also need business leaders who understand the merits of competition as well as cooperation and are willing to take individual responsibility.

As Skocpol suggests, we also need to see the positive role of government. This, I fear, would be a difficult task given recent events surrounding our entry into Iraq and Afghanistan, Guantanamo Bay criticism, and WikiLeaks (not to overlook state-level misconduct by Rod Blagojevich, Eliot Spitzer, or Anthony Weiner, to name only a few). Nevertheless, there is hope, and the Obama administration has made some progress in the area of limiting lobbyists to White House posts, increasing transparency in government, supporting Wall Street reform, and finding ways to increase public/civic participation in government. This, in addition to working across party lines, is an approach that can rebuild American faith in government—and, in the process, allow for a more meaningful dialogue surrounding healthcare reform.

# THREE

# Rebuilding the House
# of Healthcare

## The Health of the Individual versus the Health of the Group

THE GREATEST OPPORTUNITY FOR AMERICAN PUBLIC POLICY TO IMPROVE THE HEALTH OF the nation is to differentiate between the macroallocation and the microallocation of resources. When we focus on this, we recognize that there is often a conflict between the health of the individual and the health of the group and that where and when this conflict takes place it is in our interest to maximize the health of the group.

You cannot maximize all parts of a limited and fixed budget. Budgets do not tolerate abstract theories unrelated to the resources available. When we jointly pool money, as we do when we pay taxes and insurance premiums, we cannot expect unlimited benefits. No single contributor to a pool can expect a blank check in return. Any excess or unreasonable drain on the common pool comes at the expense of the others in the pool.

Scholars point out that civilization has had, largely, the growing recognition that in certain instances collective action maximizes total benefit. Humankind is prone by nature to maximize short-term self-interest, but our species has learned from millennia of experience that we can often maximize the total societal good by overcoming individual self-interest. While discussing types of goods, Elinor Ostrom writes, "Societal-wide effort is needed to effectuate these collective goods for the population."[1]

We commonly call this process "enlightened self-interest." This is an important development for humankind, because in its absence, everyone following his or her individual self-interest can leave the common good "not provided for or . . . underprovided. . . . Maximization of short-term self-interest yields outcomes leaving all participants worse off than feasible alternatives."[2]

We can often accomplish more as a group than as individuals within a group. Ostrom continues:

> The theory of collective action is the central subject of political science. It is the core of the justification for the state. Collective-action problems pervade international relations, face legislators when devising public budgets, permeate public bureaucracies and are at the core of explanation of voting, interest group formation and citizen control of governments in a democracy.[3]

Collective action and joint endeavors of the type we have developed in healthcare need rules and rule keepers. Whether designated an umpire, referee, or claims manager, someone must both set and enforce the rules of a common pool. We maximize the health of a group of individuals by considering the health opportunities available to the entire group. This is not a plea for socialism but the simple recognition that in all societies there are some functions that require collective action for the greater benefit of all. Groups of individuals often maximize social good by acting together or jointly as communities; reciprocity can be a better public policy tool than self-interest. This is as much a statement of political science as it is of sociology.

Liberal or conservative, most scholars will agree that at least some social goods must be delivered collectively. Most of us find it easier to pay taxes than to dig our own wells or sewers or to build and maintain our own roads and parks. We are safer with a fire department than with individual fire extinguishers. We can and do argue vigorously about the extent of that collective role but virtually all recognize that government does perform some functions that we cannot or would rather not do for ourselves. At some point, a world of individual outhouses doesn't work and we build sewage systems. No matter how committed we are to the market or to individualism, some functions are, by agreement, done collectively because society maximizes good by doing them together.

This reasoning clearly applies to aspects of delivering health and healthcare. Europeans, for instance, have decided through government to collectively deliver a broad range of health services; the United States has decided to collectively deliver a relatively narrow range of services. All countries have used contributions and taxes to build hospitals and fill them with medical technology and community emergency response systems. Most societies have found it in their mutual benefit not only to fund hospital emergency rooms and community clinics for the medically indigent but also to deliver a significant amount of healthcare by government. If not government, then we use insurance to share risk. This varies in the mechanism used and the degree, but the entire developed world has found a way to collectivize all or part of the risk of bad health.

Victor Fuchs has observed, "The divergence between what is beneficial for the individual and what is beneficial to the society as a whole is the key element in the current healthcare debate." How do we reconcile this divergence? Government tries to do the best it can with available resources, but it cannot blindly fund the cumulative total of all decisions that the healthcare providers find ethical or even appropriate. Public policy, after all, never promised unlimited reimbursement.

## Making Competition Work in Healthcare

CONTROL OF COSTS THROUGH MARKET COMPETITION HAS BEEN DIFFICULT TO ACHIEVE in healthcare. There are many opinions on why it has not worked, but numerous commentators point out that consumers of healthcare feel no economic pain because they are insured and thus do not feel the normal economic restraints. Ninety percent of hospital costs and two-thirds of physician fees are paid for by insurance. We pay, but not out of pocket. Economists tell us that we do not shop for what we do not pay for directly. By reducing the out-of-pocket costs of healthcare, insurance companies have also increased demand. Additionally, as experts remind us, insurance companies were set up to pay for healthcare, not to purchase it efficiently, thus they do not move easily or efficiently toward effective cost containment. They too often create administrative barriers rather than reasoned cost containment. Bottom line: there were, until the last ten years, few effective restraints on the providers of healthcare. For most of American medicine, we pay no price for excess and get no benefit from denying ourselves anything.

Paul Starr puts it this way:

> No one in the system stands to lose from its expansion. Ultimately, the population over whom insurance costs and taxes are spread has to pay. But it is too poorly organized to offer resistance. The obvious defect in this system is the absence of any effective restraint.[4]

A second reason that competition fails to control healthcare costs is that there is an asymmetry of information between doctor and patient, which makes it difficult to rely on the market one patient at a time. When we are sick, we don't know what is wrong with us or what we need—that's why we go to the doctor. Individual patients are thought to have no bargaining power over providers; we pay whatever they ask, and we do whatever they say.

Our insurance companies historically have been ineffective at managing costs. As one health expert, Lynn Etheredge, stated:

> We have chosen to "insure" healthcare rather than "manage" it. Our current system is a management failure on the part of private and public sectors alike. The traditional US health insurance company was not designed to negotiate payment rates, manage medical care, foster competition among providers, improve patient outcomes, or change physician and hospital practices. In the climate of ineffective accountability, health service delivery has grown as a fragmented cottage industry non-system in which a plethora of entrepreneurial

specialists and independent institutions seek their professional satisfaction, financial rewards, and patient service objectives.[5]

So one major goal of healthcare reform should be to reform the market. Productivity is one key to cost containment. We need to restructure the industry for continual productivity gain. There must be incentives for both the providers and the purchasers to improve productivity. Given the magnitude of healthcare (one-seventh of our economy) and the fact that government already funds more than half of the healthcare budget, it is naive to think that this restructuring can take place without some government action. Adam Smith himself recognized that government could be used to restructure the market. Government is already deeply involved in the healthcare market. The key is that when the government restructures healthcare, it does not rely upon government controls but upon market reform.

Market reform, like managed competition, restructures the market for health services into competing, prepaid health plans, giving providers built-in incentives to offer a standard (thus comparable) benefits package at the lowest cost. It is designed to pool businesses and individuals into insurance-buying cooperatives that will present to the citizens within their jurisdiction a selection of the best of the prepaid plans. Each citizen will choose the one that is best for him or her.

There are three major mechanisms under managed competition that are designed to moderate costs:

1. Develop an institution that will aggregate demand from consumers of healthcare. Let's call it a purchaser alliance. Armed with large numbers of consumers, this alliance will be able to demand good efficiency, quality, and pricing from providers. Unlike much of our managed care, which seeks efficiency on an individual level, a purchasing alliance is able to have enough leverage on the system to demand efficiency. It has the power to give all of its business to a certain set of hospitals, forcing others to close. By accumulating significant market power, this alliance

can demand prices from providers unthinkable in a different context.

2. The alliance will present to all employees a set of health plans that compete among themselves on the basis of price, quality, and access. The alliance may offer, for instance, ten plans, and the employee picks the one that best suits the entire family. Many times, the alliance will establish uniform guidelines, uniform benefits, and uniform rating parameters designed to help purchasers comparison shop among the various competing prepaid health plans. The purchaser/employee is thus empowered to shop for and pick the best value. The result is that all ten plans will compete among themselves to offer the most effective and efficient service at the lowest rate.

3. A capitated payment system would involve one payment for both physician and hospital. The theory here is that at least some of the plans offered will use capitated payment. Where utilized, capitation will force all providers of healthcare to focus on how other parties treating a patient utilize resources because they are being compensated from a common capitation payment. Each provider will claim its fair share, and each will act as a check on the other providers claiming a disproportionate share.

Under fee-for-service medicine, the more procedures that are carried out and the more expensive the technologies that are used, the more money individual physicians and hospitals make by charging each time they perform a service. But under the financial dynamics of a reformed system, this orientation has become a liability. A cost-effective system will value preventing illness, keep patients out of hospitals, and prevent unnecessary care. The incentives will be dramatically reversed. A filled hospital is one that can now focus on costs rather than on revenues.

There is an additional cost-control mechanism used in only some instances of managed competition. The original creators of managed competition limited the income tax exclusion that an employee now gains for employer-paid health insurance. If people know they will have to pay taxes on any increase in employer-paid health benefits, they will feel some constraint in picking and using health insurance.

It is important to understand that managed competition relies on a reformed market system—not governmental control—to achieve its efficiencies. It attempts to correct the lack of purchaser power when individuals access the system. It attempts to empower the demand side of healthcare.

## Reducing Individual Expectations: Overrating Ourselves

JACK LONDON, IN HIS CLASSIC BOOK *THE SEA WOLF*, GIVES US A METAPHOR FOR THE dilemma of modern American medicine when he describes how a cynical ship's captain reacts to a young seaman caught high up on the ship's mast during a storm:

> Do you know, the only value life has is what life puts upon itself; and it is of course overestimated, since it is necessarily prejudiced in its own favor. Take that man I had aloft. He held on as if he were a precious thing, a treasure beyond diamonds or rubies. . . . To you? No. To me? Not at all. To himself, yes. But I do not accept his estimate. He sadly overrates himself.

It is basic human nature to "overrate" ourselves, and this is never more true than when dealing with our health. Understandably, we all value our health. For us individually, the appropriate level of care means that we want to resolve the slightest doubt about our health with the latest technology, with care performed by the best specialist in our geographic area and in the best hospital, if necessary. As health experts have long pointed out, in America, invention has become the mother of necessity. *Can do* has become *must do* if there is the slightest possibility of benefit to our health. We "need" and demand what is available, and for most of the history of American medicine, cost was not a consideration. Americans feel immediately entitled to every new procedure and innovation from the moment they hear or read about it in the media.

We are passengers on a ship that is all sail and inadequate anchor. It will inevitably steer toward more consumption of healthcare than we can afford. Many medical traditions, such as cost never being a consideration, were not designed for modern medicine when one patient can bankrupt a plan or hospital. The dynamics of overrating our individual health concerns can never be met with commonly collected funds. Human nature urges us to maximize individual benefits, and economics urge us to overspend common pools of money.

Painfully, but inevitably, we must put our individual needs within the context of other patients' needs and other social demands of a complex society. The price of our individual overconsumption in modern medicine is paid for by others in our plan or by society not getting their adequate share. In a limited pool of resources, overtreating A is the equivalent to undertreating B. We overrate ourselves at the expense of our fellow passengers.

The core of a managed care system is to maximize responsibly the overall health of each member within the limits of available resources. The health plan, like government, has a different focus and role from a physician or patient. Health insurance and health plans have a narrower role than government, but this role still must be broader than the physician-patient focus. The focus of a plan must be the health of the group of subscribers, not always the individual subscriber. The health plan has a duty to a different moral unit than the physician. In a world of limited resources, one cannot simultaneously maximize the health of each individual and the health of the group.

Individuals paying out of pocket for their own health services can buy whatever they want. They are constrained adequately by the normal laws of economics. Both health plans and government, however, must treat everyone in a program with due process and equal protection. Inevitably they must set limits. Their moral duty is to the total group. That means, inevitably, each individual's demands on the system must be weighed against the demands of other people in the plan.

> The crux of the matter, then, is how much emphasis should be placed on the individual characteristics of each patient and how much should be placed on common characteristics shared among a population of patients.[6]

Healthcare plans cannot and should not be blind payers of all doctor-patient services. They are partners in health with a necessarily broader viewpoint. There will always be a gap between what we desire and what those who distribute limited funds estimate we need.


## Healthcare and the Courts

GUIDO CALABRESI WARNS OF THE DIFFICULTY IN WEANING THE AMERICAN PUBLIC from an entitlement mentality in his book *Tragic Choices*:

> It is a dramatically different world than we have comfortably come to know. It will intrude upon values that society has come to think of as fundamental, of benefits than constituencies have come to think of as their right, and redefine as luxuries some things that people have come to see as necessities. We must attempt to make these choices in ways that do as little violence as possible to our moral and social traditions.[7]

I have been fighting all my political life to cover the medically indigent with basic healthcare. I believe, however, it is a strategic mistake to assert that healthcare is a right or a human right. I believe this argument is well intended but a public policy mistake. I do not think its proponents have thought through all the implications of pushing this goal.

Rights are defined and interpreted by the judicial system. A right trumps all other categories of social spending. It is the language of courts developed in an adversarial process. It would be a mistake to demand that healthcare be declared a right. Even if it were achieved, it would be counterproductive to society's well-being.

Third-party payers pay for the vast majority of healthcare. Whether government or an insurer, whoever allocates these dollars will have to set priorities on how they maximize health within those limited resources. Every year there will be a different answer as technology and science enlarges our medical options and possibilities. For what benefits do we pay or not pay?

Rights are not an effective way of determining either who or what is covered. We cannot allow one social good to crowd out all the other social goods. As one expert put it:

> How can a state that lacks the resources to provide everyone who needs it with . . . renal dialysis, or a heart transplant, claim to be giving full effect to the right to health services? With the public's seemingly insatiable appetite for healthcare, how can any state reasonably recognize a universal right to services? Such acts of recognition would mean signing a blank check.[8]

Society has to balance not only the needs within the healthcare system, but also all social needs. You cannot make comparisons between the many social goods a society must allocate using the legal system. We need nuanced and comprehensive policies that compare and trade off among a great number of social needs. The language of rights or the province of courts does not advance allocating finite resources over infinite needs. If we make healthcare a right, we put it in position to crowd out all other social spending. Rights are adversarial and individual; health policy has to balance both who is covered and what is covered. It has to say both yes and no. The judicial system is too blunt an instrument to weigh and balance either within the healthcare system or among total social needs.

We can and should provide basic healthcare to all citizens, but this should be done through the legislature and not the courts, and it should be done as a matter of good social policy, not by playing the trump of rights.

## Expanding Healthcare's Moral Universe

I WOULD ARGUE AGAINST THE BILL THAT ADDED A PRESCRIPTION DRUG BENEFIT TO MEDI-care. Let me make this argument. Public policy is filled with unmet needs. The agony of serving in office is that there are so many important needs and no way to meet them all. No matter how much you care, needs go unmet. As Victor Fuchs has said:

> The hardest choices in life are not those that must be made between good and evil. The most difficult choices are those that force a decision between good and good. As Isaiah Berlin has written, "The need to choose, to sacrifice some ultimate values to others, turns out to be a permanent characteristic of the human predicament."[9]

The budget of every country in the world allocates limited resources among multiple needs. Rationing has always been with us and always will be. As one expert, Norman Daniels, puts it:

> Rationing, therefore, is an integral component of our health care system, although we euphemistically call it by other names, for example, cost sharing, preexisting condition limitations, or simply "uncovered" services. In many respects, there is little difference between these mechanisms and the existing policies in other countries that are openly acknowledged to ration care. It is not a question of whether rationing exists, but of what form it takes.[10]

Once government starts to play a role in healthcare, it has to prioritize needs. This is being done worldwide. The method varies, but all set limits. We are fooling ourselves when we do not admit that we ration. We, in fact, limit healthcare in one of the cruelest ways that any nation can limit medicine—by simply leaving people out of the system.

We can give compassionate and comprehensive healthcare to all our citizens, but we cannot give everything. We shall have to decide among the many things we can do in modern medicine what we ought to do with our limited resources to build a just society. The sooner we admit that we can't do everything, the sooner we will be able to maximize limited funds.

In a world of limited resources, we cannot explore the best use of our resources, the so-called opportunity costs of each dollar, unless we set priorities on what we can afford. We must start a community dialogue about how we can put our healthcare dollars to the highest and best use. It is an inevitable dialogue, and we ought to make a virtue out of necessity.

In 2003, Congress approved an expansion of Medicare to include prescription drugs. With our army of medically indigent who have no healthcare, should we have enriched the benefits of the one group already insured with federal money? Wouldn't it have been better to cover those citizens without any health coverage?

Public policy is a world of multiple unmet needs. The question isn't whether this new benefit is needed by Medicare recipients or beneficial to the elderly, but it is a question of priorities. Whose claim in a world of needs is most deserving for the next fungible taxpayer dollar we have available to spend? The question is not what social programs do we as a nation need. There is much unmet need; the question is, what do we need next?

Metaphorically, Congress was faced with an auditorium filled with 284 people. Of those people, 40 didn't have any health insurance and 40 more were significantly underinsured. Yet 38 of those present, the oldest but also those with the most assets and disposable income, had a fairly comprehensive health insurance policy that covered them for fee-for-service medicine. Many members of Congress decided that America's health priority was to tax the remaining 200 of those people in the auditorium, most of whom were insured but in managed care, in order to provide prescription drugs for all the 38 million elderly who already had and have, as a group, excellent health insurance coverage.

Social Security, Medicare, and Medicaid are perhaps the best antipoverty programs ever passed and still keep up to half of our elderly out of poverty. But today we are living much longer and have significantly fewer children, and Medicare is projected to go broke not far into the future. It was not wise to create an expensive new entitlement; the national priority should have been covering citizens without any health coverage.

There is another argument against a universal drug benefit for all over the age of 65. As a demographic, the elderly are not a monolith. True, the poorest people in America are elderly widows but the richest people in America are also elderly widows. Do we really need to subsidize both categories from the pockets of working Americans? In the late 1990s, more than $200 billion of federal entitlements were paid to people over 65 who had other retirement income of more than $50,000 a year.

## A Social Good but Not a Right

WE ARE JUDGING MUCH OF WHAT WE DO AND EXPECT IN HEALTH WITH AN UNSUSTAINABLE yardstick. No matter how we organize and fund healthcare, we will find that our medical miracles have outpaced our ability to pay. It is hard to change our thinking after years of blank-check medicine—but necessary. The price of modern medicine is to decide what to cover among the smorgasbord of treatments currently available. This is painful, but unavoidable.

There is a Gresham's law to language in which we dilute or diminish the meaning of important words by overuse and overextension. *Rights* is one such word, desperately important but prone to overuse. If we are to successfully change public policy, we must take great care in our use of language and strategy. A just society has many needs that cannot and should not be reduced to rights. Rights are ultimate values that a society must protect at all costs. They are our society's ultimate thou shalt nots.

But if everything is a right, nothing is a right. We can easily dilute the important meaning of this word by claiming idealistically that all good things are rights. It is a good-hearted mistake but still a mistake.

A decent and just society is a structure with many important pillars. Healthcare is one of those pillars, but so are education, justice, welfare, decent infrastructure, and a livable environment. My generation has been mesmerized by the concept of rights because the concept was so useful in expanding freedom and justice. But rights are not a universal tool applicable to every social need. Beyond being laudable goals, they are not achievable in the world of public budgets.

There is a great difference between a negative right and a positive right. You have a right to worship your God, but government doesn't have the enabling function of building you a church. You have a right to free speech, but government doesn't have to buy you a newspaper or time on television. You have the right to vote, but not to a ride to the polls. Social policy must take great care in turning rights into entitlements.

Such a concept may even antagonize those who believe in a politically achievable social safety net. I do not want the courts telling the legislature that an individual has a right to an MRI when there are kids without schoolbooks. Rights interfere with safety nets. By attempting to achieve the social optimum, they make it harder to achieve a decent minimum. The rights concept adds nothing to the wrenching process of choosing among many valid needs.

## The Collective Health of the Group

IT IS VALID TO DEBATE HOW MUCH OF HEALTH AND HEALTHCARE WE WANT TO DELIVER collectively. Yet once we choose government or insurance as an institution to deliver healthcare, we must recognize that something radical has taken place. When we chose common or pooled funds, we change the rules. However, medical culture continues under the old assumptions. Expectations linger. Americans want more healthcare as consumers than they are willing to pay for as taxpayers or premium payers. Public goods and common pools are not distributed under the same rules as the market distributes private goods. Healthcare funded half by public funds (taxpayers now fund approximately 50 percent of healthcare) is not a do-no-harm world; it is not a world where cost is not a consideration. Public policy must weigh and balance multiple needs. Public policy is a world of trade-offs, of balancing interests, of winners and losers. Neither public policy nor insurance can maximize individual self-interest.

We can improve our individual health by cooperating to distribute health insurance and tax monies and examining how to keep a community or group healthy. Just as the health of the public requires tools that collectively keep us healthy (sewers, water systems, and so forth), the public can also benefit from delivering some allopathic medicine by focusing on the health of the group rather than on the health of the individual and by considering and evaluating the health hazards to the group rather than the hazards to the individual. We can maximize health and resources by asking what strategies maximize health for the group. We can fund larger benefits for the group by not maximizing marginal medicine to individuals. It is counterintuitive but correct.

Public policy and insurance distribute a limited pool of resources to Americans who have practically unlimited expectations. When we assume unlimited resources, we pay no price for excess and get no benefit from denying ourselves anything. But assuming limited resources require us to look at the big picture, we recognize that we can maximize the health of the group only by making trade-offs and setting priorities. *Trade-offs* sounds like a compromising term that will limit both our options and our health. The opposite is true.

Coverage criteria are the primary legal mechanisms by which plans, physicians, and members can reach agreement on how the members' money should be used to maximize the members' health. It is to ensure that plans do not waste their members' money on nonmedical, ineffective, or harmful practices.

When we pool taxes or insurance dollars, we have to ask, What maximizes the health of those who make up the pool? It requires a broader social vision than fee-for-service medicine. Public funds must maximize the health of the public:

> Every medical decision is a spending decision and a judgment about whether an intervention is "medically necessary" carries with it a decision about whether it warrants coverage. Physicians and patients who agree to be bound by these plans' cost containment protocols have made a contractual commitment that cannot be dismissed merely because of inconvenience.[11]

No policy makers should ever take the Hippocratic oath. The same applies to health insurance companies. They have a duty to maximize health, but we cannot expect them to do no harm.

Reinhard Priester states, "Providers should not do everything that maximizes benefit in an individual patient, since doing so may interfere with the ability of other patients to obtain basic services, rather, providers should treat each patient with a full range of resources as is comparable with treating patients yet to come." Those words sound harsh to those who have blindly assumed a world of unlimited resources where cost is not a consideration. This perspective is strikingly different from what we are used to. We should seek to start a new dialogue on how to evaluate those who manage group resources.

Healthcare has gone from a cottage industry to a series of integrated delivery systems. It has gone from open-ended funding to a world of budgets and cost controls. A world of budgets is, by definition, going to be more restrictive than a world of unlimited funding. It will require the American public to adopt new expectations and new yardsticks in choosing their health providers. The skill of the physician continues to be of immense importance, but it is no longer the only consideration. We must also ask which system allocates its funds in the most healthful manner. As you hold a college to a different standard than you use in picking an individual professor, so also must you find new standards to judge the total healthcare group. The individual doctor and individual professor are important, but your main evaluation is of the system.

Physicians try to push up the ceiling of care given to an individual patient; systems try to first build solid floors for the group. Physicians' microallocate, while systems macroallocate. If the system finds, as Southern California Kaiser has, that it can save twice as many women for two-thirds of the money by concentrating mammography on women between the ages of 50 and 70, isn't that better than giving mammograms to all women in their 40s? The money saved could be used for other, more health-producing strategies.

American healthcare and the expectations of the American public have developed during the most massive transfer of wealth into one sector (healthcare) that history has ever seen. This has distorted our view and masked the necessity to make some hard choices. We have had seemingly endless pools of money allowing us to do everything for everybody who was lucky enough to be in the system. As health expert William Mercer said, "Health insurance coverage was seen as a credit card whose charges never came due, and 'more' care was always 'better' care." Unfortunately, that system is bankrupting us and is unsustainable.

We cannot have unlimited healthcare by paying limited taxes and insurance premiums. Pooled resources are always limited resources. Once we honestly admit that healthcare is not an open-ended system, the whole dialogue changes. When we share a finite pool of funds, my excesses contribute to your inadequacies. Again, David Eddy notes:

> It is important to understand that even on the relatively rare occasions when a particular member disagrees with the plan's coverage decision, responsible plans are still trying to act in the best interest of its entire membership. If selected individuals can get coverage for particular treatments that do not meet the criteria agreed to in the contract, they are siphoning resources from the pool available to provide care to other members.[12]

All stakeholders can't possibly optimize in a world of limited resources. The challenge is to make people understand that this is not bad news but actually in their best interest.

# New Challenges: Obesity

OBESITY. THE WORD RESONATES DEEPLY FOR US AMERICANS. WE ARE INUNDATED with graphic images, various TV shows, countless books, autobiographies, and . . . *warnings*. The Centers for Disease Control and Prevention (CDC) categorizes an adult with a body mass index (BMI) of 30 or higher as obese. Body mass index is the ratio of one's body weight in kilograms to the square of body height in meters (i.e., weight divided by height squared). The below table provides a sample guideline:

**FIGURE 13.** BODY MASS INDEX

| BMI | Normal | | | | | | Overweight | | | | | Obese | | | | | | | | | | Extreme Obesity | | | | | | | | | |
|---|---|---|---|---|---|---|---|---|---|---|---|---|---|---|---|---|---|---|---|---|---|---|---|---|---|---|---|---|---|---|---|
| | 19 | 20 | 21 | 22 | 23 | 24 | 25 | 26 | 27 | 28 | 29 | 30 | 31 | 32 | 33 | 34 | 35 | 36 | 37 | 38 | 39 | 40 | 41 | 42 | 43 | 44 | 45 | 46 | 47 | 48 | 49 |
| Height (inches) | | | | | | | | | | | | Body Weight (pounds) | | | | | | | | | | | | | | | | | | | |
| 58 | 91 | 96 | 100 | 105 | 110 | 115 | 119 | 124 | 129 | 134 | 138 | 143 | 148 | 153 | 158 | 162 | 167 | 172 | 177 | 181 | 186 | 191 | 196 | 201 | 205 | 210 | 215 | 220 | 224 | 229 | 234 |
| 59 | 94 | 99 | 104 | 109 | 114 | 119 | 124 | 128 | 133 | 138 | 143 | 148 | 153 | 158 | 163 | 168 | 173 | 178 | 183 | 188 | 193 | 198 | 203 | 208 | 212 | 217 | 222 | 227 | 232 | 237 | 242 |
| 60 | 97 | 102 | 107 | 112 | 118 | 123 | 128 | 133 | 138 | 143 | 148 | 153 | 158 | 163 | 168 | 174 | 179 | 184 | 189 | 194 | 199 | 204 | 209 | 215 | 220 | 225 | 230 | 235 | 240 | 245 | 250 |
| 61 | 100 | 106 | 111 | 116 | 122 | 127 | 132 | 137 | 143 | 148 | 153 | 158 | 164 | 169 | 174 | 180 | 185 | 190 | 195 | 201 | 206 | 211 | 217 | 222 | 227 | 232 | 238 | 243 | 248 | 254 | 259 |
| 62 | 104 | 109 | 115 | 120 | 126 | 131 | 136 | 142 | 147 | 153 | 158 | 164 | 169 | 175 | 180 | 186 | 191 | 196 | 202 | 207 | 213 | 218 | 224 | 229 | 235 | 240 | 246 | 251 | 256 | 262 | 267 |
| 63 | 107 | 113 | 118 | 124 | 130 | 135 | 141 | 146 | 152 | 158 | 163 | 169 | 175 | 180 | 186 | 191 | 197 | 203 | 208 | 214 | 220 | 225 | 231 | 237 | 242 | 248 | 254 | 259 | 265 | 270 | 278 |
| 64 | 110 | 116 | 122 | 128 | 134 | 140 | 145 | 151 | 157 | 163 | 169 | 174 | 180 | 186 | 192 | 197 | 204 | 209 | 215 | 221 | 227 | 232 | 238 | 244 | 250 | 256 | 262 | 267 | 273 | 279 | 285 |
| 65 | 114 | 120 | 126 | 132 | 138 | 144 | 150 | 156 | 162 | 168 | 174 | 180 | 186 | 192 | 198 | 204 | 210 | 216 | 222 | 228 | 234 | 240 | 246 | 252 | 258 | 264 | 270 | 276 | 282 | 288 | 294 |
| 66 | 118 | 124 | 130 | 136 | 142 | 148 | 155 | 161 | 167 | 173 | 179 | 186 | 192 | 198 | 204 | 210 | 216 | 223 | 229 | 235 | 241 | 247 | 253 | 260 | 266 | 272 | 278 | 284 | 291 | 297 | 303 |

*Source:* **National Heart, Lung, and Blood Institute; National Institute of Health; US Department of Health and Human Services**

For an individual who is 5 feet tall (or 60 inches), a normal BMI would require a weight range from 97 to 123 pounds. An overweight person would weigh between 128 and 148 pounds. From 153 to 199 pounds, the individual would be considered obese. Any weight above this limit would be categorized as extreme obesity. Although somewhat crude, BMI provides a quick and easy gauge of obesity.

Most certainly, BMI is not the only tool to gauge someone's health fitness. In fact, the CDC cautions that BMI does not measure body fat and individuals with high BMIs *may not* be obese or even overweight—for example, some athletes. Other measures of body fat include skin-fold thickness using calipers, underwater weighing/displacement, and dual-energy X-ray absorptiometry (DXA).

The National Heart, Lung, and Blood Institute assesses an individual's weight and health risk using three measures: (1) BMI, (2) waist circumference (to gauge the amount of abdominal fat), and (3) other obesity risk factors, such as high blood pressure or amount of physical inactivitiy

A logical question is, What is so worrisome about obesity? A large body of research from the National Institutes of Health suggests that obese individuals are at greater risk for diabetes mellitus, cardiovascular diseases, hypertension, and certain cancers. In addition, obese individuals diagnosed with non-insulin-dependent diabetes mellitus (NIDDM) may also suffer from complications, such as diabetic ketoacidosis, diabetic coma, diabetic retinopathy, and diabetic neuropathy. Symptomatic gallstones are also a concern, since obese individuals are at greater risk of developing gallstones due to higher cholesterol levels. As for cancer, Graham Colditz suggests that approximately "11 percent of breast cancers among postmenopausal women are attributable to obesity."

Besides disease, "excess bodyweight is associated with negative effects on longevity, disability-free life-years, quality-of-life, and productivity."[13] Obese individuals are more likely to suffer from mobility and physical restrictions, less likely to partake in certain activities due to arthritis, and more likely to miss work.

## Obesity Trends

ACCORDING TO A 2010 STUDY BY CYNTHIA OGDEN ET AL., MORE THAN ONE-THIRD of American adults were obese during 2007–2008. These scholars report some interesting findings. For one, obesity prevalence is "generally similar at all income levels; however, among non-Hispanic black and Mexican American men, those with higher income are more likely to be obese than those with low income." For women, this does not apply. Higher-income women are less likely to be obese; however, the majority of obese women are not from low incomes. In terms of education, women with college degrees are less likely to be obese. In an earlier section of this book, I highlighted the connection between health and education. Perhaps obesity is less prevalent among educated women because this group takes more health-related courses and/or applies more of this knowledge when making dietary choices. Nevertheless, Ogden et al. found that "between 1988–1994 and 2007–2008, the prevalence of obesity increased in adults at all income and education levels." At this point, we should note an earlier study, in 1992, by Katherine Flegal et al. These scholars' data from "representative samples of US men and women 18–34 years of age show little variation in mean body mass index (BMI) over a 20-year period from 1960–1980." In other words, issues surrounding obesity have been of concern for nearly 50 years and not just recently. The below figure summarizes some of these findings and provides the prevalence of obesity from 2005 to 2008.

**FIGURE 14.** PREVALENCE OF OBESITY AMONG ADULTS AGED 20 YEARS AND OVER, BY POVERTY INCOME RATIO, SEX, AND RACE AND ETHNICITY: UNITED STATES 2005–2008

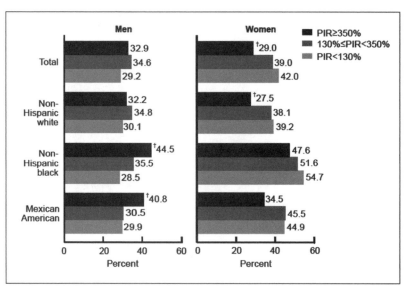

†Significant trend.
NOTES: PIR is poverty income ratio. Persons of other race and ethnicity included in total.

*Source: Ogden CL, Lamb MM, Carroll MD, Flegal KM. Obesity and Socioeconomic Status in Adults: United States 1988–1994 and 2005–2009. NCHS data brief no 50. Hyattsville, MD: National Center for Health Statistics.*

The following figures provide a historical perspective. Figure 15 shows a considerable increase in obesity prevalence for both men and women from 1988–1994 to 2005–2008. For men and women with a poverty-income ratio above 350 percent, we see an increase of more than 10 percent. Equally worrisome, this increase occurred for those with relatively higher incomes. More specifically, for men and women with a poverty-income ratio *less than* 130 percent, we see nearly an 8 percent increase. Figure 16 reveals an increase in the prevalence of obesity at all education levels for men and women. This substantial increase among men and women with some college education seems uncharacteristic—for both genders, the change exceeds 14 percent, and this is the largest for any education category. Once again, one would *not* expect such a dramatic increase for those with relatively greater education.

**FIGURE 15.** PREVALENCE OF OBESITY AMONG ADULTS AGE 20 YEARS AND OVER, BY POVERTY INCOME RATIO AND SEX, FROM 1988–1994 AND 2005–2008

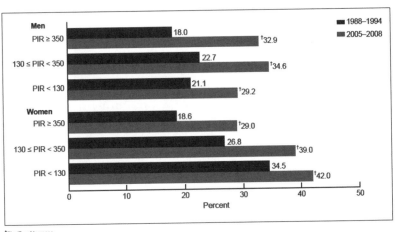

†Significant increase.
NOTE: PIR is poverty income ratio.

*Source:* Ogden CL, Lamb MM, Carroll MD, Flegal KM. Obesity and Socioeconomic Status in Adults: United States 1988–1994 and 2005–2009. NCHS data brief no 50. Hyattsville, MD: National Center for Health Statistics.

**FIGURE 16.** PREVALENCE OF OBESITY AMONG ADULTS AGE 20 YEARS AND OVER, BY EDUCATION AND SEX, FROM 1988–1994 AND 2005–2008

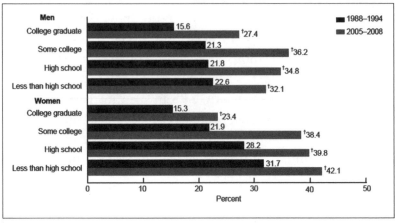

†Significant increase.

*Source:* Ogden CL, Lamb MM, Carroll MD, Flegal KM. Obesity and Socioeconomic Status in Adults: United States 1988–1994 and 2005–2009. NCHS data brief no 50. Hyattsville, MD: National Center for Health Statistics.

# Economic Costs of Obesity

NEARLY TWO DECADES AGO, IN 1992, GRAHAM COLDITZ WROTE AN ARTICLE IN THE *American Journal of Clinical Nutrition* examining both the indirect and direct health costs attributed to obesity. His estimates show nearly $11.3 billion for non-insulin-dependent diabetes mellitus, $22.2 billion for cardiovascular disease, $2.4 billion for gallbladder disease, $1.5 billion for hypertension, and $1.9 billion for breast and colon cancer (in 1986 dollars). Colditz's estimates are conservative since the calculations do not include musculoskeletal disorders or other deaths attributed to obesity.[14] As I discussed earlier, the US population will be older in the upcoming few decades. This is important to note because Y. Claire. Wang et al. claim that "about half of these costs [$14 billion of the $28 billion] would be incurred by individuals 65 years and older (covered by the publicly funded Medicare programme)."

Cost estimates from E. A. Finkelstein et al. in 2010 shows that obese patients sustain 46 percent increased inpatient costs, 27 percent increased physician visits and outpatient costs, and an astonishing 80 percent increased prescription drug costs, as compared to normal-weight individuals. These scholars also show costs due to absenteeism and presenteeism or lost productivity. When compared to men of healthy weight, grade III obese men (BMI is greater than 40) cost the "equivalent of 1 month of lost productivity and cost employers $3,792 per year." Excess body weight may also impose additional costs due to other disorders, such as benign prostate hypertrophy, infertility, asthma, sleep apnea, and congenital anomalies from maternal obesity. A 2009 article by L. Trasande et al. in *Medical Care* shows that an obese diagnosis for pregnant women is associated with "significant increases in length of stay (LOS), charges, and costs" and higher frequency of Cesarean sections. More specifically, these scholars suggest an increase of nearly $2,015 in charges and $1,805 in costs.

The following figure shows the past and projected prevalence of overweight. Wang et al. suggest that if obesity trends continue, three of four Americans will be overweight or obese by 2020. This will not be unique to the United States. Other countries, notably England, face a similar crisis. Australia also faces a dire predicament; the prevalence of obesity there is expected to increase substantially during this decade. Korea seems to be the only country with some control on weight—although it will also experience a slight increase.

**FIGURE 17.** PAST AND PROJECTED PREVALENCE OF OVERWEIGHT
(BMI GREATER THAN 25)

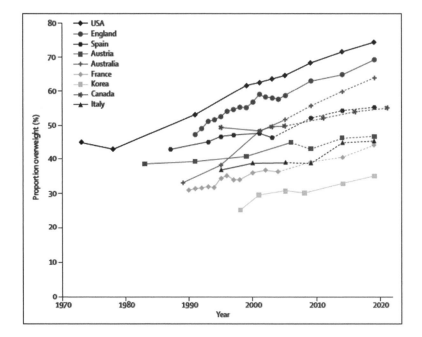

*Source:* Reprinted from *The Lancet*, vol. 378, no. 9793, Y Claire Wang, Klim McPherson, Tim Marsh, Steve L. Gortmaker, and Martin Brown , "Health and Economic Burden of the Projected Obesity Trends in the USA and the UK," 815–825, © 2011, with permission from Elsevier.

The below figure shows projected healthcare costs based on two trends. Panel A depicts the *historic trend*, which is based on twenty years of trend data (as early as 1988) with an accelerated obesity trend. Panel B depicts the *current trend*, which is based on more recent data (as early as 2000) with a leveling obesity trend. Despite this more optimistic trend, the United States would still see costs of more than $40 billion for treating obesity-related diseases by 2030.

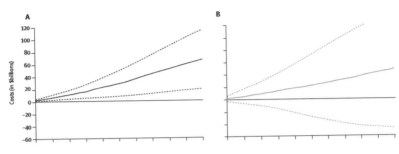

Dashed lines represent 95 percent Confidence Interval.

*Source:* Reprinted from *The Lancet*, vol. 378, no. 9793, Y Claire Wang, Klim McPherson, Tim Marsh, Steve L. Gortmaker, and Martin Brown, "Health and Economic Burden of the Projected Obesity Trends in the USA and the UK," 815–825, © 2011, with permission from Elsevier.

# Costs of Childhood Obesity

ADULT OBESITY IS ONLY ONE AREA OF CONCERN. ALTHOUGH "RECENT DATA SUGGEST that the prevalence of obesity among children did not increase during the period 1999–2006," a 2009 study by L. Trasande et al. "detected a near-doubling in hospitalizations with a diagnosis of obesity between 1999 and 2005 and an increase in costs from $125.9 million to $237.6 million (in 2005 dollars) between 2001 and 2005." These scholars also find that Medicare pays a large fraction of hospitalizations related to obesity. The following figure provides a time line of the number of hospitalizations and charges from 1999 to 2005.

**FIGURE 19.** TRENDS IN HOSPITILIZATIONS AND CHARGES AMONG CHILDREN AND YOUTH AGES 2–19, WHERE OBESITY WAS A PRIMARY OR SECONDARY DIAGNOSIS, IN 2005 DOLLARS, 1999–2005

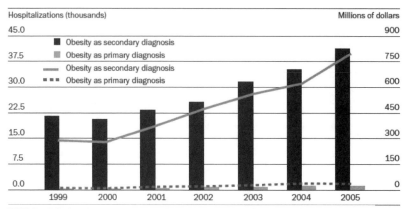

NOTES: Hospitalizations (thousands) are represented by bars and relate to the left-hand y axis. Millions of dollars in hospitalization charges are represented by the line graph and relate to the right-hand y axis.

*Source:* Copyrighted and published by Project HOPE/Health Affairs as Leonardo Trasande and Samprit Chatterjee, "The Impact of Obesity on Health Service Utilization and Costs in Childhood," *Health Affairs* (Millwood). © 2009, vol. 17, no. 9, 1749–1754. The published article is archived and available online at www.healthaffairs.org/."

**FIGURE 20.** CLAIMS BASED ON OBESITY DIAGNOSIS AND COSTS, AMONG CHILDREN AND ADULTS, IMB CORPORATION, 2008

| Population | Number | Percent of total | Mean allowed dollars |
|---|---|---|---|
| **Children 18 and under** | | | |
| Non-obese | 51,422 | 99.0 | $1,640 |
| Obese[a] | 369 | 0.7 | $2,907 |
| Type II diabetes[b] | 77 | 0.2 | $10,789 |
| | | | |
| **Adults** | | | |
| Non-obese | 204,613 | 87.0 | $4,520 |
| Obese[a] | 6,249 | 3.0 | $8,889 |
| Type II diabetes[b] | 25,278 | 11.0 | $8,844 |

Note: Claims are allowed gross claims. [a]Obese: International Classification of Diseases, Ninth Revision (ICD-9) codes 278.XX (primary, secondary, tertiary—overlap with diabetes other disease). [b]Type II diabetes: ICD-9 Codes 250.XX.

Source: Copyrighted and published by Project HOPE/Health Affairs as Martin J. Sepulveda, Fan Tait, Edward Zimmerman, and Dee Edington, "Impact of Childhood Obesity on Employers," *Health Affairs* (Millwood). © 2010, vol. 29, no. 3, 513–521. The published article is archived and available online at www.healthaffairs.org.

**FIGURE 21.** HEALTH SERVICES UTILIZATION BY CHILDREN AGE EIGHTEEN, IMB CORPORATION, 2008

| Type of service | Units per 1,000 claimants | | Ratio, obese to non-obese |
| --- | --- | --- | --- |
| | Obese (n = 369) | Non-obese (n = 51,422) | |
| Emergency room | 439 | 337 | 1.3 |
| Surgery related | 881 | 489 | 1.8 |
| Behavioral health visits | 1,566 | 533 | 2.9 |
| Physician care (excludes routine physicals) | 7,843 | 6,469 | 1.2 |
| Physical therapy | 1,585 | 1,013 | 1.6 |
| Lab/pathology | 6,778 | 2,899 | 2.3 |
| Prescription drugs | 5,482 | 3,814 | 1.4 |
| Outpatient facility | 98 | 52 | 1.9 |

Notes: Allowed number of claims, self-insured plans. Obese: International Classification of Diseases, Ninth Revision (ICD-9) codes 278.XX range (278.00, 278.01, 278.1, 278.2, 278.3, 278.4, 278.8).

Source: Copyrighted and published by Project HOPE/Health Affairs as Martin J. Sepulveda, Fan Tait, Edward Zimmerman, and Dee Edington, "Impact of Childhood Obesity on Employers," Health Affairs (Millwood). © 2010, vol. 29, no. 3, 513–521. The published article is archived and available online at www.healthaffairs.org.

The scholars found that obese children under 18 years of age utilize various health services at a much higher level. For example, behavioral health visits by obese children are nearly triple that of non-obese counterparts. Surgery-related visits are nearly double for obese children, as is use of outpatient facilities. Since families, employers, and society must pay for the direct and indirect costs, IBM developed a program to encourage parents to take an active role in their children's exercise and nutrition. The Children's Health Rebate gives "parents incentives to promote behavior changes and family activities in food management, physical activity, and personal screen time." The voluntary program guides employees toward various family-specific activities for twelve weeks. Upon successful completion, the employee receives a $150 cash rebate. The following table summarizes the key results.

**FIGURE 22.** REPORTED IMPROVEMENTS BY IMB CHILDREN'S HEALTH REBATE EARNERS, 2008

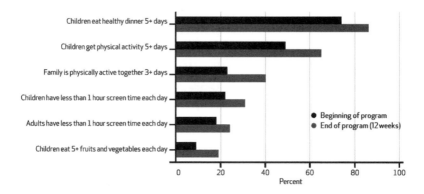

*Source:* **Copyrighted and published by Project HOPE/Health Affairs as Martin J. Sepulveda, Fan Tait, Edward Zimmerman, and Dee Edington, "Impact of Childhood Obesity on Employers," *Health Affairs* (Millwood). © 2010, vol. 29, no. 3, 513–521. The published article is archived and available online at www.healthaffairs.org.**

IBM claims this program "provided positive outcomes for both employees and the company. Employees who took part in the focus groups after participating in the program expressed high levels of satisfaction," and many reported that "involving all family members in health behavior change was the most valuable part of the program." This is most certainly a step in the right direction if we are to control obesity, improve the quality of life for children, and maintain healthcare costs. Families, employees, and the community must work collectively and, in the process, develop some type of support network. Simply passing the responsibility to the individual or government is not enough given our dire situation.

## The Corner Place with Governor Lamm

### For Policy Makers and Policy Analysts

On a sleepy spring afternoon in March 1984, during my third term as governor of Colorado, in response to a question at a small meeting of health lawyers in the back room of a Denver hospital,

I took exception to the term *right to die* used by a questioner. I observed that death is not an option and that instead "we have a duty to die." To be precise, here are the words transcribed from my press secretary's tape recorder.

The real question gets into, then, high-technology medicine. We have a million and a half heart attacks a year. Every year in the United States we have a million and a half heart attacks. Six hundred thousand of them die. How many Barney Clarks can we afford? How many heart transplants can we afford?

You know, we at least ought to be talking about that. I think that we're rapidly approaching the day where medical science can keep people alive in hospitals, hooked up to tubes and things, far beyond when any kind of quality of life is left at all. But yet, medical science can keep us alive.

It seems to be that it's at least a question society ought to be talking about, What are the ethical implications?

A terrific article that I've read . . . one of the philosophers of our time, I think, is a guy named Leon Kass. Has anybody seen his stuff? He's just terrific. In *The American Scholar* last year, he wrote an article called "The Case for Mortality," where essentially he said we have a duty to die. It's like if leaves fall off a tree forming the humus for the other plants to grow. . . . We've got a duty to die and get out of the way, with all of our machines and artificial hearts and everything else like that and let the other society—our kids—build a reasonable life.[15]

When we left the meeting, I asked Sue O'Brien, my excellent and savvy press secretary, if there would be any news coming out of the event. "I doubt it," ventured Sue, who would spend ten hours a day for the next three weeks putting out fires I had just unwittingly ignited.

The next morning I arose at 4:30, as is my wont, and worked on a book I was soon to have published. At 7:00 I came down in my running clothes and asked the state patrolman to open up the security gates. I was aware of the distant ringing of many phones.

"Governor, don't you want to see the newspapers?" asked the state patrolman. "Thanks, no. I'll read them later," I responded.

I walked out into the front yard of the governor's residence and got halfway to the automatic gates, which were lumbering open, when it struck me that the patrolman on duty, who had become a friend of the family's (as is always the case with people whom you share a significant part of your life with), looked worried. It was clearly not like him to ask me if I wanted the papers when I was on my way to run. I returned and asked for the papers.

There on the front page of *The Denver Post*, right below the fold, was the headline "Gov. Lamm Says Elderly and Terminally Ill Have Duty to Die." He then handed me a thick stack of phone messages on a spindle. Death seemed more near; I felt I was reading my obituary.

Besides the predictable press calls were an array of citizens' calls (we kept the governor's residence listed in the phone book) ranging from support to threats. One caller urged me to get tested for Alzheimer's disease, a diagnosis he said he had long suspected in me.

You cannot imagine the shock wave that hits a governor's office when there is a crisis like this. One of the joys of being governor is that your staff is so much more than employees; they work long and hard hours out of a mixture of dedication, ideology, and a camaraderie that makes them more a team than a staff.

The team often seems to mirror the mood and fortunes of the governor. When things go well, the team has a wonderful esprit de corps. Jealousies are present but minimal. The mood has the buoyancy of a group that knows it is doing important and valuable work. The climate is sunny, but my governorship had been through storms.

I was elected governor at 39 and had never run anything larger than a small law office. I had been preceded by twenty-four years of Republican governors, and I had deeply offended many in the business community by opposing the Olympics coming to Colorado and a significant number of other people by my sponsorship of liberalized abortion. Being governor is a sink-or-swim job, and I no sooner took office than I started to sink. Most of my problems were self-imposed as I struggled to appoint cabinet and staff, forge agendas, move into the governor's residence, and be a husband and father to two small kids. I could seem to do nothing right.

The staff was loyal, always hardworking, but glum. They handled critical telephone calls and acquainted themselves with the business of government, but a dark cloud hung over the whole office. Bumper stickers appeared on the streets that referred back to my campaign: Lamm Could Walk the State, but Can't Run It. I slowly learned to swim, and the whole wonderful staff sparkled with dedication and purpose. Ten years later, it looked like those terrible times were coming back.

Sue greeted me at the office with an invitation to *Good Morning America* and a bushel basket of press inquiries. My chief of staff had been getting calls from Democratic legislators and party officials. My administrative assistant was juggling an incessantly ringing telephone, and my security people seemed especially attentive lest some octogenarian pummel me with a cane.

Coincidentally, a group of Colorado senior citizens was meeting at a church across from the capitol. My staff quickly arranged an appearance, and by 11:00 am, with a flock of TV cameras and press, we walked across the street. I asked myself, After trying mightily to get the press interested in some of Colorado's most serious problems, how could a few thoughtless words cause this much commotion?

I was put immediately at ease by a warm reception and had a meaningful dialogue with thoughtful seniors. The chairman tried to help me off the hook: Did I mean *right to die*? "No," I responded. "Death is not an option or a right, but the fate of all of us." And so it went for an hour.

That morning I started hearing a theme that, surprisingly, I kept on hearing. A large number of seniors believed that they did have a duty to die. On the way out, one lady handed me a piece of paper with a quote that Thomas Jefferson wrote to John Adams as both neared death: "It is reasonable that we should drop off and make room for another growth. When we have lived our generation out, we should not wish to encroach upon another."

That theme kept coming up in the following weeks. A significant minority of the letters we received believed in the misquote and told me not to back down. I have come to agree with it, but now, as a senior citizen myself, I have the bona fides to venture an opinion of a group I myself am in.

Two days after the article appeared, I was on the *Today Show* and a number of other national programs. Three days later, President Reagan was asked in a press conference whether he agreed with Governor Lamm that seniors had a duty to die. To his great credit, he responded that he understood that that wasn't exactly what was said.

Slowly, the news tide ebbed, and life returned to normal. Hundreds of editorials were written, columnists praised and blamed, and one newspaper titled its article "Lamm to Elderly: Drop Dead."

Lessons learned from this: First, the press overall is committed to truth and free inquiry. *The Denver Post*, while never admitting it was in error, did clarify my remarks and wrote a laudatory editorial saying wasn't it wonderful to have a thoughtful and provocative governor. Second, America was ready to have a dialogue on death and dying. Within a few years, most states (today, all 50) had living-will legislation or the equivalent. Third, if you are sincere and don't back down, the public admires a certain level of candid outspokenness. Both while I was in office and after, a large number of people came up to me and said to the effect, "I don't always agree with you, but I sure admire you for speaking out forcefully and candidly."

The fourth lesson is not so positive: Politicians should stay away from sensitive subjects. You can understand why politicians tend to be prosaic and boring. Science advances when a scientist states a new truth, inviting and welcoming criticism and correction. Truth advances by the yin and yang of argument. But in politics, every new idea, every new program proposed, and even every new word and phrase risks uncontrollable controversy and defeat. None of the feedback loop that science is built upon can be counted on in politics; if you give your opponent an opening, you risk political death. Even though the polls showed I suffered no damage from the misquote, the obvious message to the political establishment was "Stay safe and boring."

# The Book Nook with Dr. Sharma

## Trade-Offs: Short-Run Costs versus Long-Term Benefits

SOME HEALTH POLICY SCHOLARS HAVE SUGGESTED THAT HIGH-END TECHNOLOGY HAS driven part of our increasing healthcare expenditures. A 2007 special report by the Kaiser Family Foundation, *How Changes in Medical Technology Affect Healthcare Costs*, indicates that healthcare spending has grown just under 10 percent per year since 1970.[16] In terms of raw figures, annual spending on healthcare approximated $75 billion in 1970 and reached $2 trillion in 2005. As of 2009, total spending was close to $2.5 trillion.

Although accounting for the costs of improved technology is difficult, economists have used indirect approaches to show that a substantial increase in healthcare costs can be attributed to technological change. Readers interested in undertaking a preliminary and historical approach to this relationship between healthcare cost and technology by examining books by Daniel Callahan or William Hanson. In *Taming the Beloved Beast: How Medical Technology Costs Are Destroying Our Health Care System*, Daniel Callahan presents some cogent arguments for and against medical technology. More specifically, he claims that technological innovations (in this case, a technology bubble) are increasing medical costs at an alarming rate and that this cannot be sustainable for the organization of healthcare. Equally important, these skyrocketing costs present ethical challenges that require us to reconsider our values surrounding equity and progress.

In contrast, *The Edge of Medicine: The Technology That Will Change Our Lives* by William Hanson extols medical innovation. This book combines patient medical histories with current and future technological breakthroughs—marvels such as medical robots, nanotechnology, implants, and proton beam therapy. *The Future of Medicine: Megatrends in Health Care That Will Improve Your Quality of Life* by Stephen C. Schimpff also focuses on the technological revolution in medicine. This book provides a fairly comprehensive assessment by discussing biomedical research laboratories (genomics, stem cell), computational and engineering laboratories (imaging, nanodevices), and complementary medicine (ancient traditions). The most fascinating aspect of this book is its exploration of how medicine will be practiced in the future: that is, it will change from detection/treatment to prediction/prevention.

Of course, each of these books evoke wonder and amazement. They also spark some to ask, Who is going to pay for this billion-dollar machine and the million-dollar treatment? And a few will also press further: Is it even necessary? I agree that medical innovation comes at a cost. More specifically, a hefty short-run cost. However, we should pay this cost in those instances in which there is a substantial long-term benefit. As a case in point, consider heart attacks, one of the leading causes of death in the United States. During the 1970s, coronary artery bypass surgery was a risky and costly procedure and the primary option for some individuals. By 1990, angioplasty and revascularization became available.[17] And by 2000, cardiologists could also use drug-eluting stents and offer beta-blockers, statins, and aspirin as long-term management strategies. The innovations in cardiac medicine have been so effective during the past three decades as to decrease mortality from myocardial infarction from nearly 345 per 100,000 to 186 per 100,000.

Unfortunately, not all treatments or procedures show such promise. I was enrolled in the doctoral program in public policy at the University of North Carolina from 2006 to 2009. During Christmas break of 2008, I visited my parents in Chicago. My mother had been ill for quite some time, and I was under the impression that she was suffering from pneumonia. Since her lungs were filling with liquid, my father would regularly take her to the hospital for drainage. I returned to Chapel Hill in January with the hope that my mother's condition would markedly improve. As I was preparing for my upcoming dissertation defense, my older brother called with the most shocking news I ever heard: "Mom has cancer and she has two weeks to live." I took the first flight from Raleigh-Durham International to O'Hare.

Shortly after landing, I swiftly maneuvered through one of the world's busiest airports, and my brother took me to Elmhurst Memorial Hospital. I was in tears the whole time. I tried to conceal my sadness as I approached my mother's room, but the situation was too difficult, and I cried on my mother's lap. We were all grief stricken, and my brother, my sister-in-law, and I were also in shock. My parents had decided not to inform us of my mother's condition on the grounds that we would worry too much and the possibility that my mother would have a good prognosis from the previous chemotherapy session.

The next day, I met the oncologist and he confirmed the poor prognosis. The cancer had spread so rapidly and so extensively during the past few weeks as to leave my mother less than a month of life. My father, desperate to keep my mother alive, adamantly requested Avastin, a drug used in chemotherapy. My brother and sister-in-law also spoke to the oncologist and demanded the treatment. Shortly after lunch, the doctor informed us that he was prepared to begin the treatment if that was truly what we desired. I asked him about the long-term benefits and what the outcome would be for someone with my mother's particular condition. He quietly explained that she could potentially die during the administration phase, but if she pulled through then the likelihood of surviving a year was very small.

When I heard this, my doctoral research training kicked in full force, and I began scouring medical journals and bulletins for information. I discovered that Avastin did not show much promise despite approval by the Food and Drug Administration. In fact, the outcomes were so poor that I wondered how the heck this thing could even be offered as treatment. To be candid, I was outraged that Avastin would even be an option. I explained these findings to my father and the rest of my family. Naturally, they had a hard time accepting this dire news because they so desperately wanted my mother to live, and this very expensive drug was a seen as a miracle. Slowly but surely, my family realized that no drug would help my mother, and we had to accept the fact she was going to die. None of us wanted this, and all of us had hoped to use the most up-to-date treatment and the most sophisticated technology to keep my mother alive.

The latest and the greatest treatment is what we all desire, but this should not be an option if the costs exceed the benefits.

A very expensive treatment (whether paid for privately or publicly) that provides the individual no more than a few additional years of life—not to mention the possibility that such a treatment would *not* significantly improve quality of life—may not be the best option. Yes, this is a personal decision, but these are the types of decisions we must also discuss as a society. As Daniel Callahan suggests, we need to reconsider our values surrounding medical innovation.

My mother passed away on January 27, 2009. Nearly two years later, Avastin was removed as a treatment option for breast cancer. I am so glad we decided not to undergo treatment with this ineffective drug. Not only would the outcome have been grim, but we all would have endured several months of anguish. Because of this experience, I am critical of certain drug manufacturers and appalled that our system would approve drugs with dismal results based on clinical trials. Nevertheless, I believe in the value of research and a collective desire to improve our human experience—our *global* human experience. Thus, we should continue to invest heavily in research and development, seek medical innovation, and reward creativity. But we also need to be aware (both as individuals and as a society) that not all ventures, no matter how expensive they are, will yield promise.

FOUR

# Rethinking the Institutions
# of an Aging Society

## Rethinking Entitlements

HERE ARE SEVERAL OPTIONS THAT ADDRESS THE AGING OF AMERICA'S POPULATION, THE growth in federal entitlement spending, and the realities of healthcare in the future. None of them is pleasant, and all have dangerous political implications. But as Pete Peterson once said, "Trying to make sense of the federal budget without taking on entitlements is like trying to clean your garage without moving the Winnebago." Some or all of the following must be done:

### 1. Social Security

- Raise the retirement age to reflect America's changing demographics. Currently, the retirement age to receive full Social Security benefits is scheduled to rise to age 67 for those born 1960 or later. The eligibility for Medicare is currently age 65. In order to account for the fact that Americans are living more than sixteen years longer now than when Social Security began, we should accelerate the plan to change the Social Security retirement age and increase the age to 70. People would still have the option to retire early at age 62, but with reduced Social Security benefits in exchange. Similarly, the eligibility age for full Medicare benefits should be increased to 70. Seniors would be eligible for health insurance at 65 but would be required to pay a greater share of their costs if they choose to enroll in Medicare early.

- Reduce benefits for upper-income persons. One way to control the explosive growth of entitlements is to limit the benefits to upper-income individuals who do not rely on benefits as a source of income. The Concord Coalition has proposed a comprehensive means test for all entitlements, including Social Security and Medicare. Under this proposal, payments to individuals would be reduced on a sliding scale starting at a family income level of $40,000. For every $10,000 that a family earns in excess of $40,000, benefits would be reduced by 10 percent. Benefits would not be reduced by more than 85 percent. In this way, every citizen would be eligible for some modest return on earlier payroll taxes.

- Reducing entitlement payments to upper-income families is not only fair, it is one of the only realistic ways to control entitlement spending. As a nation, we can no longer afford to make annual Social Security and Medicare payments of $81 billion to 6 million citizens with incomes over $50,000 a year. Furthermore, as our demographics continue to change, the amount of benefits going to middle- and upper-income individuals will increase dramatically. If we want important programs such as Social Security and Medicare to survive at all for those who really need them, we simply must learn to set limits for those who do not need the benefits.

- Limit cost-of-living adjustments. Under current law, monthly benefits paid to Social Security and federal and military retirement beneficiaries are automatically increased annually for changes in the cost of living as measured by the consumer price index (CPI). At one time, the Boskin Commission estimated that the CPI was overstated by as much as 1.5 percent, but the Bureau of Labor Statistics has incorporated some of the suggestions of the Boskin Commission into the

CPI formula. However, we still have the option of reducing cost-of-living adjustments for beneficiaries whose benefits are above the thirtieth percentile of benefits paid. All beneficiaries would continue to receive a cost-of-living adjustment. Those below the thirtieth percentile would receive the full cost-of-living adjustment. Beneficiaries above the thirtieth percentile would receive a flat dollar amount.

• Develop a personal investment plan. Countries that save and invest faster have more rapid improvements in the standard of living for their citizens. In the United States, private savings have dropped from more than 10 percent of the economy in the 1970s to less than 4 percent today. With a personal investment plan, participants would be allowed to choose to invest their funds in vehicles currently permitted by IRAs, including stocks, bonds, and mutual funds. The hope is that this would allow participants to earn higher rates of return on a portion of their Social Security payroll tax contributions, shift funds from US Treasury securities to productive investment in the economy, introduce more flexibility for retirement decisions, and increase personal and national savings.

It is imperative that we start taking a long-term view of the challenges our aging society poses to the United States. Pension systems have what actuaries call a long tail. The consequences of today's decisions on pension policy have an impact on our children and grandchildren.

## 2. Medicare

When Medicare Part A program (which is essentially hospital insurance) was enacted, it was a self-supporting system, financed solely by payroll tax contributions. Today, the average enrollee's past contributions pay less than 40 percent of the cost. As a result, the average enrollee collects benefits equaling approximately three times the amount contributed during his or her working life. But even that has not relieved the burden of healthcare for seniors. Despite the fact that Medicare was originally constructed as a program that would ease the burden of older persons when paying for healthcare, Medicare beneficiaries now pay a greater percentage of their incomes for out-of-pocket healthcare expenses than they did before Medicare was enacted in 1965.

The Medicare Part B program (which is essentially insurance for doctor bills) has undergone similar changes. When Part B began, the enrollee and the federal government each paid 50 percent of the costs. Today, the federal government pays 73 percent of Part B costs; that share is projected to increase to 92 percent by 2030. To address these inequities, we should:

- Index the Part B premium to program costs and restore the 50 percent share of the costs once paid by enrollees.

- Raise the Part B deductible from $100 to $300 in addition to indexing it.

- Add a 20 percent coinsurance payment for clinical lab services and home healthcare services costing in excess of $10.

- Add a graduated Part A premium for beneficiaries with incomes 200 or 300 percent above the poverty level.

### 3. Redefining Retirement

America must begin to think about aging and retirement in different terms. The tradition of turning 65 and immediately retiring is both unaffordable and outdated. As Americans live longer, we are capable of being productive and active members of society well into our eighth and ninth decades. We must begin a national dialogue about options for people beyond age 65. Aging experts and many senior advocates agree that contentment and longevity in old age are greatly enhanced by some form of productive employment. We must examine opportunities for semiretirement and phased-in retirement. If we are to raise the eligibility age for federal benefits, we must help employers find ways to keep seniors in the workforce. We also must adapt our federal retirement systems so that working beyond 65 is an incentive rather than a disincentive. In short, we must, as a society, abandon the idea that turning 65 automatically means retiring to Florida. If we are going to live longer, then we are simply going to have to work longer.

## Redrawing the Ethics Map

LATE IN THE THIRTEENTH CENTURY, MARTIN OF TOURS, ALONE AND COLD, WAS RIDING his horse through the deepening night toward the medieval walled city that was his destination. Right outside the city gates, he came across a cold and starving beggar. In an act of charity, which resulted in him being sainted a few hundred years later, he took half his cloak and half his dinner and gave them to the beggar. It was clearly the ethical thing to do and has served as an example of Christian charity for centuries.

Yet Bertolt Brecht, in one of his plays, raises this fascinating question: What if instead of one cold and starving beggar there were 50 or 60 or 100? What is the ethical choice now? What does the ethical person do? There is no way or reason to choose one among the many cold and starving beggars. Moreover, it is hard to ethically know what to do other than perhaps say a prayer for them all as you ride past them into the city or to devote one's life to public service.

We need new metaphors for our ethical analysis. This parable raises one of the dilemmas that the world is faced with in twenty-first-century healthcare: demands vastly exceed the resources available. We are confronted with a new set of realities, and we must develop a new set of values, a new set of institutions, and a new way of looking at public policy if we are going to resolve the implications of this brave new world.

The code of medical ethics forms a map to a world I am not totally comfortable with and a map I cannot always follow. It describes a very different world than the world of public budgets. The funding of healthcare is a different moral universe than the ethics of delivering healthcare one patient at a time, thus the existing ethics map is leading to increasingly unethical public policy results. Medical ethics need to be revised if they are to serve as meaningful guides to the future. We need a new ethics map.

Most medical ethics were formed assuming that resources were unlimited and that the sole issue was the interest of the individual patient. Indeed, some of the best ethicists claim that

> [m]edical ethics become interesting and relevant only when it abandons the ephemeral realm of theory and abstract speculations and gets down to practical questions raised by real, everyday problems of health and illness. . . . It is real-life, flesh-and-blood cases which raise fundamental questions.[1]

Laudatory words, but this is not the language of public policy, which writes a check for half the costs. Robert Veatch, one of the superstars of health ethics, has himself moved beyond his own quote. Public policy cannot blindly follow and must not be controlled by an ethical code that is developed one individual at a time, ignoring or underestimating costs. Such a procedure violates the first rule of public policy: maximize the public good with limited funds. Constructing a public budget is a process of trade-offs and priority setting seeking the maximum public good. Indeed, Rudolph Klein suggests from the British experience, "It is unethical . . . to ignore costs."

The moral unit of a physician is the patient, the moral unit of the health plan is all the members of the plan, while the moral unit of public policy is all citizens. It took John Kitzhaber, a physician and politician, to point out to a disbelieving nation that as an officeholder he was responsible both for those covered and those not covered. He could consider not only an individual child's need for a transplant but also the state's duty to all of the medically indigent. He was not arguing for a two-tier system; he was trying to maximize limited public funds in the only healthcare program for the medically indigent the state had legislated. It made more ethical sense to him, as a public policy maker, to start out covering all the medically indigent and ration what was subsidized, not who was subsidized. As David Eddy noted in *The Journal of the American Medical Association,* "If you followed Kitzhaber as governor of Oregon, would you suggest to the legislature that they remove half of the medically indigent from the Medicaid roles but give everything possible to the remaining 50 percent?"

Public policy doesn't have the luxury of focusing on one policy area (or one funding program) in a vacuum. Everything is on the table, all the time. As General George Marshall said during World War II, "When deciding what to do, one is also deciding what not to do." I cannot adequately express my frustration at sitting in a hospital ethics meeting, agonizing over whether to recognize a living will and knowing that within blocks there are medically indigent citizens with very restricted access to any healthcare. Doctors, on their way to work, drive on streets filled with potholes. They drive past crumbling schools in an inadequately policed part of the city while engaged in a profession that will never let cost be a consideration in healthcare.

How can our society possibly spend $2.5 trillion, more than half of which comes from government funds, and not look at the larger issue of total societal well-being? How do we know that the social goods we buy with those dollars are worth buying compared with society's other needs? How do I justify $150,000 for each year of life gained by hospital CPR measures, knowing that in my world $150,000 funds five schoolteachers for a year? Can you give me the password to the moral code that maintained Karen Ann Quinlan on life support in a state that doesn't bother to cover 16 percent of its citizens with basic healthcare? How can a government that has an inadequate infrastructure and kids without vaccinations use public funds to maintain anencephalic infants? This weighing process is a matter of total societal priorities, not a matter of abstract medical ethics.

For 50 years the medical profession has ignored the World Health Organization's definition of health as the "complete physical, mental, and social well-being, and not merely the absence of disease or injury." Should public policy also ignore it? Perhaps a doctor, as a patient advocate, cannot make such a definition work, but public policy has a duty to maximize health, not healthcare. At least public policy has more comprehensive tools to follow such a definition. We know now that healthcare is not the only way, or even the best way, to keep a population healthy.

If there is a conflict between the total social good and the good of an individual, public policy is sworn to uphold the public interest. Public policy has to place the one-way streets, the fire stations, the television towers, the garbage dumps somewhere. The only way a public budget can operate is by setting priorities and making trade-offs. But it isn't only public budgets that must maximize good. Contributive justice demands that I not make unreasonable demands on any jointly collected funds.

All a priori thinking developed around individual cases and assuming unlimited resources must be rethought. Health policy is too important to be subcontracted to health providers. Their map does not contain enough territory. Said another way, total social justice cannot be built out of medical ethics. It is a whole different moral geography.

If, as Robert Blank argues, "the primary goal of the health-care system should be to maximize the collective health of society, not individual medical benefit," we will have to do more than adjust at the margins. We will need a fundamental change in medical culture, medical ethics, health law, and public expectations.

Public policy demands some public interest imperative where we test the ethics of specific individuals against an ethical whole. The sum total of our ethical choices, "real-life, flesh-and-blood cases," has given us an unethical system. We see the trees but not the forest.

Barney Clark, the first recipient of an artificial heart, did not exist in a vacuum but as a member of a society with myriad public needs. Humana's budget for the artificial heart was approximately the same as what the world spent eradicating smallpox. Clark didn't exist in isolation but in an empirical world of many needs and demands. We cannot optimize a person's care and ethically deal with the whole society. Barney Clark was entitled to his rights as an American citizen, but these rights cannot include publicly subsidized longevity at all costs.

Most ethical theories are built around individuals and do not take into consideration the cumulative impact of those ethics.

Unavoidably, there is a conflict between individual goods and societal goods. No person sees his or her air conditioner as the cause of the power outage. Every driver in a traffic jam pleads not guilty. We cannot optimize the solution for both the driver and society. Similarly, you cannot optimize the health of the individual and the health of a group.

No system can have an ethical code built around individuals that requires a standard of conduct that cumulatively will destroy the system. A code of individual-based ethics must be sustainable over time and over the entire population, and it cannot harm or destroy the system it was created to serve.

This is not as harsh as patient advocates might think. It reflects not an absence of caring but a broader definition of caring. The artificial heart becomes less important when we lift our eyes from Barney Clark's bedside and view total unmet social needs.

Public policy is a different world from that of the bedside. Medical ethics can educate and enlighten, but they cannot control public decision-making. Medical ethics may protest but ultimately must yield. They provide important information but not the full picture. Making optimal social policy is terra incognita that must be mapped anew.

## Ethical Standards/Fiscal Realities

OUR NATION CANNOT HOPE TO SOLVE THE PROBLEMS FACING HEALTHCARE UNTIL WE synchronize our social policy with our medical ethics. To government policy, rationing is not only individual denial of services but also societal denial of access. Public policy cannot define its moral course an individual at a time. Public policy requires methods of assessing health needs that look not at individuals but at the broader health-producing possibilities for society. It must quantify need cumulatively and relate that need to the real world of limited available resources. It is a valid and necessary role to ask, How do we keep an entire society (group) healthy? According to authors Howard Brody and Franklin G. Miller,

So long as all the physician had to offer the patient was his own time and advice and a few herbs and powders, both medicine and society could comfortably claim that the physician's duty of fidelity was owed solely to the individual patient. When physicians can, with the stroke of their pens, literally bankrupt the community, the community may no longer be able to tolerate that view of the physicians' duty.

Ethical values that depend on the resources of others cannot be separated from fiscal realities. In budgeting, it is not so much a question of right or wrong, or good or bad; it is instead a question of better or worse. Which funding strategy buys us the most health?

Conflicts will inevitably develop between what the physician-patient relationship demands and what the third-party payer can reasonably justify paying. These are not so much differences in caring but differences in roles and perception. What makes a brilliant physician also makes a physician a less-than-objective allocator of resources. The physician sees an individual patient's need but not the relative need of the group. The insurer sees the total need but doesn't have to look a patient in the eye and say no. There are both different roles for and different yardsticks used by those who pay and those who deliver care in a modern, resource-intensive healthcare system.

A large number of unexplored moral issues applicable to the macroallocation of health resources are questions more of social policy than of medical ethics. How do we set priorities and make trade-offs in a world of limitless needs?

> The distinction between macro-allocation and micro-allocation of resources is crucial. More traditional bio-ethical analysis may well clarify the micro-allocation issues, but it is inappropriate at the macro-allocation level and therefore misses the point. . . . The allocation of health care resources is best understood as a political rather than an ethical issue.[2]

Physicians must recognize the validity of the role of third-party funder, public or private, and recognize (even when disagreeing) that their advocacy for a particular patient can't always be funded. Haavi Morreim calls them "necessary health partners." Physicians must recognize that a part of their culture seems to make morally obligatory the practices and behaviors that increase health spending without regard to others who have jointly contributed to the common pool or without regard to other social priorities that get crowded out by the incessant demands of healthcare. Physicians can be expected to advocate for, but not necessarily receive, all required resources they think beneficial to their patients.

## Controlling Healthcare Costs

HOW DO NATIONS CONTROL HEALTHCARE COSTS? IT IS A QUESTION THAT IS ON EVERY-one's mind. We know how to expand coverage, but too little is being said about the hard choices that a society must make if it is to control costs. Politicians speak grandly about national health-care reform but speak little about what will actually be neces-sary to control the volcanic pressures pushing healthcare costs upward.

I have looked at various healthcare systems around the world, with a particular emphasis on how nations control health-care costs. Predictably, there are myriad subtleties involved, but let me list some of the major methods.

### 1. Limit Supply Side of Healthcare
Supply in healthcare (i.e., doctors, specialists, hospitals and beds, medical technology) seems to encourage demand. Most countries limit the amount of healthcare infrastructure that has to be paid off by society. Most European nations strictly limit the number of doctors. Great Britain admits 4,150 students to medical school every year, expecting 4,000 to graduate. This is a carefully calcu-lated number (though some think too high) of how many addi-tional doctors will be needed in a given year. The United States likely has a surplus of doctors. Studies estimate that every doctor

we add to our society adds some $400,000 to healthcare costs. Doctors, like lawyers, seem to generate their own market share. Excess doctors mean excess costs.

Most industrialized nations also restrict the number of doctors trained as specialists. Most countries train only 20 percent as specialists; the United States trains approximately 60 percent of its doctors as specialists, though this is slowly changing. Most countries put a high premium on good primary healthcare doctors and try to make sure that all of their citizens have good primary care. Family doctors, not fancy machines, maximize a nation's health. In the United States, the prevailing ethic at medical schools is specialization because that is where the money, challenge, and large reputations are found. Overtraining specialists is a very expensive endeavor for a society. Denver, for instance, has twice as many cardiologists as Health and Human Services estimates show are needed. Local health experts admit that there are too many cardiologists (and other specialists), and this is an expensive luxury that has to be paid for by society.

Most industrialized nations put strict limits on hospitals, hospital beds, and medical technology. They recognize that once the hospital beds are in place, there is strong pressure to fill them. Even though the United States actually has a smaller number of hospital beds per capita than most nations, we still find significant surplus of beds in many parts of our country. The United States seems to have a 7-Eleven approach to hospitals: we want a hospital on every corner filled with every marvelous machine and open twenty-four hours a day. This is a terribly expensive luxury.

Similarly, the United States is filled with superfluous medical technology. Colorado (population 5 million) alone has more MRI machines than does Canada (population 32 million). We also have more open-heart surgery units than Canada—most of them underutilized and all of them expensive. The more that I look at healthcare, the more that I recognize the need to control supply. It is like an airline trying to operate profitably with only 50 percent of the seats filled; it does not make any economic sense.

## 2. Limit Malpractice Suits

No nation has as many lawyers per capita or is as litigious as the United States. Colorado, for instance, ranks fourth in the nation in lawyers per capita. This is not an asset. The legal system thus hangs over everything that we do in Colorado, especially urging doctors and hospitals to leave no stone unturned in their diagnoses. True, doctors often overreact and use this as an excuse, but the combination of real and imagined fear of lawsuits is dramatically driving our healthcare costs. It is beyond question that defensive medicine adds a substantial cost to US healthcare.

## 3. Reduce Bureaucracy and Administrative Costs

Comparing the United States' healthcare system to other healthcare systems, the question of bureaucracy and administrative costs soon emerges. The United States spends somewhere between 18 and 24 percent of its healthcare dollars on bureaucracy, while other nations spend around 10 percent. When I became governor in 1975, I was told every health transaction in America generates, on average, ten pieces of paper. It seems clear that today, the electronic equivalents do likewise as the doctors and hospitals sort out which of the 1,500 insurance companies, 50 states, and federal agencies they have to bill for a patient's services. The American healthcare system has been adding two or three administrative workers to the system for every additional doctor. This is both expensive and unnecessary. Other nations have found a variety of ways to cut down administrative costs. This often means dramatically reducing the number of insurers or even eliminating insurance companies' role in healthcare. The United States spends an incredible amount of money for underwriting costs, salesmen expenses, advertising, claims adjusters, claims administration, and bureaucracy, which other nations avoid altogether. An NBC special on healthcare showed a 300-bed hospital in Bellingham, Washington, that had 42 billing clerks. A few miles away in Vancouver, British Columbia, a 300-bed hospital had one billing clerk. American doctors and hospitals have by far the highest overhead in the world.

### 4. Allow No Direct Access to Specialists

Most countries use the primary healthcare doctor as a gatekeeper and do not allow people to self-refer to specialists. All nations that have looked at this recognize that people should have direct and immediate access to good primary physicians, but that it is the physician-gatekeeper who should forward the patient on to an expensive specialist. This, of course, is also one of the secrets of Kaiser Permanente and other managed care organizations in the United States. Citizens do not suffer a health burden with this restriction. Studies by Robert H. Miller and Harold S. Luft show that, though it may be a little more time consuming, people who are treated through managed care are every bit as healthy as people who are treated by the best fee-for-service medicine. Countries that use physician-gatekeepers are every bit as healthy as we are.

### 5. Use of Ancillary Personnel

Most nations form a health team that serves a group of citizens. While the physician is the key team member, these nations make maximum use of community nurses, pediatric nurses, and other ancillary personnel. I was amazed to see in England a chemist (pharmacist) checking blood pressure and giving a pregnancy test. When doctors do not have a pecuniary interest in themselves performing every task, a society is able to much better utilize other professionals and save itself considerable money. It is estimated, for instance, that 80 percent of the tasks a pediatrician does can be done with equal skill and excellence by a child healthcare associate.

### 6. Avoid Perverse Incentives of Medicine

Most countries pay their doctors on a capitation basis or salary as opposed to fee-for-service medicine. Contrary to what many American doctors will tell you, the doctors in these foreign countries would, for the most part, have it no other way. They have much higher rates of satisfaction within their profession than do American doctors. They have not lost their clinical freedom. On the contrary, they argue (I think correctly) that American doctors, who have to clear so many things through insurance companies, have many more restrictions put on their clinical freedom than do most European healthcare systems.

Perverse incentives still dramatically drive American healthcare. Despite managed care, too many doctors and hospitals get paid on a piecemeal basis. The more they do, the more they get paid. The temptation to overtreat is obvious, but there are other perverse incentives. American citizens are not careful purchasers, because they generally are spending free dollars, which have their genesis either in insurance companies or in the government. Lawyers hang over the whole system like a sword of Damocles. And, last but not least, employees for the most part do not pay income taxes on their employer-paid health benefits, encouraging more and more compensation in this form, thus inserting yet another perverse incentive into the system.

### 7. Limit Long-Shot Medicine

When you look at the American healthcare system, you soon find that no other system spends as much on futile health expenditures. We spend nearly 30 percent of our healthcare dollars on the sickest 1 percent of people. While I do not mean to imply that all of the money is wasted, virtually every doctor will admit that much of it is. I was very impressed in England that people who really needed healthcare received it, but doctors there did not practice the kind of long-shot medicine that we do in America, where we too often substitute activity for good judgment.

England will give chemotherapy to every treatable cancer, but it does not spend a lot of time treating a metastatic cancer just because it will make the patient and family feel that something is being done. There are, of course, many other examples. England does less than half of the X-rays per capita than the United States does (and uses only half the film per set of X-rays). Yet while I was there, the Royal College of Radiologists estimated that 20 percent of the X-rays performed in Great Britain were clinically unnecessary. What does that say about the United States' system, which dramatically over–X-rays many people, either as a protection from malpractice or as a convenience for physicians who do not want to check with another doctor for X-rays already taken?

Similarly, it is estimated that 40 percent of our lab work is simply unnecessary, and it is often performed merely because the doctor has an economic interest in a local lab.

## 8. Limit Organizational Chaos

No healthcare system in the world even approaches the US healthcare system for balkanization of delivery of healthcare. The federal government runs Medicare, while Medicaid is run by the states, though the federal government pays for approximately 50 percent of Medicaid. We have separate healthcare programs for veterans (Why do we have/need 153 veterans' hospitals?), and separate programs for dependents of our military. Fifteen hundred health insurers handle the private insurance market. This balkanization prevents any payer from getting enough leverage on the system to gain efficiencies, and massive amounts of extra overhead are engendered.

The excesses of the American healthcare system, as enumerated above (and by no means are all listed), are a national tragedy. We are taking money that we desperately need to redo our infrastructure, to educate our children, or to refurbish our industries, and we are spending it wastefully in the healthcare system. At some point, historians are going to look back at America and wonder how any society could be as reckless with its limited resources. America has no stomach for hard choices, and that may eventually bankrupt us.

# Conclusion

AMERICANS ARE THE PEOPLE OF ABUNDANCE. WALT WHITMAN CALLED AMERICA THE "land of the bulging storehouse and endless freight trains." When I entered the Colorado legislature in 1967, America was doubling its per capita wealth every thirty years. We had a substantial growth dividend every year, both to increase our standard of living and to devise new government benefits. Medicare and Medicaid were born in the era of spare-no-cost government. We deliberately started a domestic war against pollution, poverty, cancer, discrimination, and poor health in the elderly and indigent. Government could say yes without saying no. Massive transfusions of money went into healthcare and healthcare's infrastructure. But those days are long gone and unlikely to return. The march of time has given us a series of new dilemmas in healthcare, which will tax our imagination, ingenuity, and resources. Our technologies push the boundaries of the possible. We have failed to build institutions equal to the magnitude of the problems we face. In terms of our largest public expenditures, we have built systems without brakes. We cannot solve our healthcare challenges within the current dialogue and thinking. When we focus so exclusively on treating individuals with medical care, we miss many public health measures that could gain us, both as a society and as individuals, even more health. We find ourselves in a public policy catch-22, where public policy relies on a medical culture and ethical standards that are bound to bankrupt it. At the same time, it allows us to ignore the larger, more important need for nonmedical funding for other social needs. Our healthcare system allows us, indeed encourages us, to ignore the big picture. We fail to ask, With all this talk about medical ethics one individual at a time, do we have an ethical system?

No profession can claim public resources in isolation from other social needs. From a public policy viewpoint, we have built the house of ethics on an inadequate foundation. To the extent that taxpayer monies fund our healthcare system, that system must prove its worth amidst all competing social needs. Our healthcare system must be consistent with our economic realities and the survival of other social priorities. The ethics of good intentions must be grounded in economic reality. Government simply cannot write into law, nor can it base a reimbursement system on, a code of ethics developed by a profession. If we really are going to take seriously the World Health Organization's comprehensive definition of health (complete physical, mental, and social well-being), we must consider the entire public policy landscape. As the Canadian study *Determinants of Health* found, "For more than half a century the understanding that there is much more to health than healthcare has been largely ignored, despite the fact that increased spending on the formal healthcare system is no longer having a corresponding positive impact on overall population health."

The health economy is a subpart of the larger economy, and medical needs are a subpart of the total world of public and private needs. No nation or system can meet all individual needs and desires of an aging, technologically obsessed society by using pooled funds.

Our current system maximizes demand for medical services paid for with pooled resources within a system that insulates patients from the cost. No system, public or private, can allow people to consume as worried patients and fund as parsimonious taxpayers or rate payers. Someone must judge whether an intervention is a fair and reasonable expenditure of the group's limited funds.

Ultimately, no common pool of funds collected by third-party payers can be used without regard to the law of diminishing returns. If every American would get all the beneficial healthcare demanded by current medical ethics and practice, it would create an unethical society where medical care trumps too many other important social needs. Medical ethics provide no mechanism to weigh and balance individual health needs with other social or group needs. However elegantly reasoned, medical ethics cannot control the practical allocation of pooled funds.

As Henry Aaron has stated:

> But while each of us may know that the well-being of loved ones is beyond price to us, the simple fact is that society has never placed infinite value on lives—and never will. The assertion that healthcare is an unlimited right invokes the principal [sic] that rights must be honored regardless of cost. This principle is violated every day and everywhere with universal approval.

What would we suggest in a healthcare system? We agree with those people who say change in America is generally evolutionary and that we have to build on what we have. While it's not our ideal system, we would suggest all employers cover employees (those who work more than twenty hours a week) with healthcare. We would suggest tax credits for employers to help offset the economic burden. We would also require copays and thus utilize the market in discouraging marginal care. Yes, it will also discourage some isolated episodes of needed care, but we would accept that as a price of expanded coverage.

For a state or nation to cover all its citizens with modern medicine, it must (1) subsidize those who cannot afford coverage, (2) avoid free riders by compelling all citizens to pay something into the system, and (3) set limits on what healthcare is covered. Limits are painful but inevitable if we are to avoid crowding out all other social spending.

We need a new moral vision for healthcare, and we end with what we see to be the essential elements of that new vision:

1. A nation's health goal can never be, nor should it be, to fund the sum of all its citizens' individual needs. Thus, the legislature should not be limited to or controlled by the ethics of the physician-patient relationship. That relationship is important but not exclusive. Not only is it not in the public's best interest to fund everything a physician may

think will advance a patient's health, but also, when correctly analyzed, it is not in the patient's best interest.

2. Public policy should concern itself more with extending the healthcare floor than raising the research ceiling. Public policy makers must care about the health of the total society as passionately as health providers care about an individual's health.

3. Group funds, public or private, should maximize the health of the group. It is the duty of those distributing pooled money to optimize the health of all those in the pool. The doctor-patient relationship may be the most important relationship in healthcare, but it is not the only relationship. Doctors are patient advocates, but they are imperfect agents to maximize the health of a group of patients or a nation.

4. When people pool funds, they cannot maximize the amount of beneficial treatment to each member of that pool, and cost has to be a consideration when distributing those funds. We optimize the health of a group by suboptimizing the treatment of the individual. As Haavi Morreim says, "We cannot fairly insist that physicians owe to a patient resources they neither own nor control . . . we should neither expect nor permit the medical profession unilaterally to choose the values that will set the amounts and purposes for which other people must spend their money."

5. Not only is the Oregon Prioritization Plan ethical, it is unethical for a state not to have a system of priorities. Likewise, those in health plans who distribute pooled resources have an independent, ethical duty to prioritize and budget those funds to maximize the total health of the group. Governor Kitzhaber demands that we give our attention to the issues of healthcare coverage, benefits, and cost. All are important; all are interrelated. Public

policy must find a way to prioritize what benefits are covered instead of which citizen is covered.

6. We must recognize that the problem of the uninsured and the problem of cost containment are not unrelated problems but are intertwined and must be solved together.

7. We must go substantially beyond eliminating waste and inefficiency into the unpopular issues of life, death, and cost-benefit thinking. One of the toughest issues of the future is: What beneficial medicine can we ethically avoid funding? What may have been unthinkable under assumptions of infinite resources becomes thinkable in the trade-off world of finite resources. Many concepts must be reconsidered and debated anew. Does not a society owe a greater moral duty to a 10-year-old than to a 90-year-old? Should not a patient's smoking and drinking habits be weighed against the high cost of rescue procedures?

8. Life is precious but cannot be priceless. Death is always a loss, but now it is often a publicly subsidized event. There will always be ten leading causes of death no matter how brilliant our medicine. The threat to biological life cannot hijack a disproportionate share of finite resources needed elsewhere for the quality of life. People have a right to die, but it is a negative right against interference, not a positive right to a state-subsidized death regardless of cost. The postponement of death is an important value, but it must take its place among other health values.

9. We do not necessarily maximize health by maximizing healthcare. Society must better analyze and study the determinants of health for a state and nation. The most important issue for Congress to debate is not prescription drugs for the elderly but how to keep a nation healthy. What factors produce health? For this we have the benefit of a number of other countries already having considered the subject.

10. We have not adequately structured the house of healthcare. We have overbuilt and overfurnished the first floor, but most of the rest of the structure remains unfinished. There are multiple levels of ethical analysis in health policy: a legislator, a health plan provider, and a family member have different moral duties and a different moral geography than a doctor. We need different levels of ethical analyses corresponding to the various levels of moral obligation.

11. All modern healthcare must be based first on self-responsibility. We are our own best doctors and cannot expect society to cure the consequences of all our self-imposed illnesses. We have to rebuild the house of healthcare by rethinking the moral duties of each level of healthcare. The foundation of the house of healthcare is self-responsibility. The first floor is the ethics and duties of the doctor-patient relationship. The second floor is the ethics and duties of the health insurance plan whose financial and moral obligation is to the total group whose premiums make up the money under the plan's control. The third floor is the ethics and duties of the state and nation. Neither the second nor the third floor of healthcare can give the Hippocratic oath a blank check, and rationing is inevitable. We need new ethical analyses to determine the roles of the health plan provider and government and to better evaluate their fiduciary duty in the funding of healthcare. All three levels of healthcare are necessarily related but not coterminous, with rationing being unavoidable on the top two floors. Only when the American public understands this can we begin to revamp our healthcare system.

# Final Thoughts
# *by Governor Lamm*

## The Path Forward

ON NOVEMBER 7, 2012, PRESIDENT OBAMA WON REELECTION, BUT SADLY IT DOESN'T follow that Obamacare won. The polls show that only 26 percent of the public supported fully implementing the Affordable Care Act (ACA). Less than half of self-identified Democrats supported fully implementing the new law. Far more Americans want to repeal, delay, or block the law than want to implement it.

The new health legislation wasn't any more popular with the voters in 2012 than it had been in 2010 when it dragged many Democrats to defeat. Obama won in 2012 in spite of his new historic healthcare legislation, not because of it. Americans remain at best skeptical, and at worst significantly negative, about the new law. They believe, overwhelmingly, that it will increase the costs of healthcare. The road to full implementation will contain many roadblocks.

Thirty Republican governors, the majority of the US House of Representatives, and a significant minority of the US Senate oppose the new law, a coalition not powerful enough to repeal the law but powerful enough to prevent smooth implementation. Nevertheless, do not underestimate the power of incumbency or the reality of legislation in place and upheld by the US Supreme Court: the ACA has passed and is the law of the land. Time is on its side.

Let us reconstruct how the ACA came into being. In 2009, newly elected Barack Obama had a two-front war on his hands when trying to fulfill his healthcare campaign promises. Many Democrats wanted a single-payer healthcare system like Canada's, but Obama recognized that this was not politically feasible. It is often unrecognized that while Canada has a first-rate healthcare system—and one that is far more popular among its citizens than ours is here—to implement a single-payer system in the United States would require replacing the approximately $800 billion in healthcare premiums paid by employers with new taxes. The price of a single-payer system is not so much the need for additional money into the system, but paying the existing bill. A single-payer system would require shifting that $800 billion—now paid by employers—to new taxes, which clearly was a non-starter.

So what does a newly elected president do? President Obama chose a strategic and logical course. He based his proposal on two Republican ideas: Governor Romney's Massachusetts health reform and Senator John McCain's tax on Cadillac plans. He tried to get bipartisan support by using what had been Republican ideas. The President knew that all major pieces of social legislation, like Social Security, Medicare, Medicaid, and Civil Rights legislation, had in the past (and need today) bipartisan support.

In 2009, it was a card well played, but it did not work. Partisan lines in America were by then deeply drawn. Perhaps at no time since the Civil War had so wide a divide separated the two major parties. What had been a successful bipartisan effort in Massachusetts became "socialized medicine" in parts of the US Congress. It is hard to see how any other proposal could have succeeded, but you play the game with the cards you have drawn.

That said, time is on the side of the ACA. The hurricane of misinformation has abated, and people are starting to better understand what the law contains. The shame of being the only developed country without universal coverage is growing, as is the recognition that for most Americans there will be no change in how they get their healthcare and insurance. Expanded coverage is to be achieved by an individual mandate, with subsidies for those who can't afford coverage, and an employer-mandate, which helps keep most employees and their families in their existing health plans, minimizing disruption. Young adults, from the moment the president signed the bill, could remain covered as dependents on their parents' health insurance up to age 26 and denial of coverage because of preexisting conditions was prohibited, as were caps on total insurance payouts, which historically have left some desperately sick people suddenly without coverage. By the end of 2014, millions more people will have health insurance, many for the first time in their lives. America may argue about potential benefits, but once in place they are hard to displace.

The most controversial part of the ACA was and is the individual mandate. Ironically, Candidate Obama in 2008 had been against the individual mandate. But as he confronted the reality of achieving universal coverage, he recognized that, if he was going to make progress in covering America's approximately 50 million uninsured, he would have to instate a mandate with subsidies for those who could not afford coverage. No universal health insurance schemes can allow free riders who avoid paying for health insurance until they get sick. Universal coverage requires compulsion to get people signed into the system and subsidies for those who can't afford the premiums.

How can this possibly be "socialized medicine," as his opponents claim, when the Heritage Foundation, a conservative think tank, originally promoted the individual mandate as a free-market solution to increase health insurance coverage? The Heritage Foundation argued this was the "conservative" way to expand coverage. So President Obama adopted in his healthcare proposal an individual mandate that had its roots in a conservative foundation and that a Republican governor in Massachusetts implemented. None of this saved his proposal from the constant, vitriolic criticism that he was promoting the government take-over of healthcare. But its conservative pedigree helped the ACA get passed.

# Where do we go from here?

LET US SUGGEST THAT WE HAVE NO REAL CHOICE. THE AFFORDABLE CARE ACT WILL not be repealed. It has passed and been upheld by the Supreme Court, and implementing regulations have been issued. Most states are in the process of setting up the new market mechanism called exchanges. The ACA itself has great promise, and we anticipate that most of the opposition will eventually shrink away, excepting only pockets of hard liners. Implementation will be a constant fight, but as the country better understands what is in the new legislation and how it works, it will be accepted, even if it does not become popular. There will be many federalism challenges when some states choose to set up their own exchanges and other states have exchanges imposed upon them, but these are normal problems of implementation. The framework of the ACA seems more than adequate to allow the nation to evolve its way into a workable and universal healthcare system.

The great challenge of this legislation will develop around the word *affordable* in the Affordable Care Act. However difficult, the problem of adding millions additional people to the system is just part of the larger challenge of cost control. We have a new law, but can we afford it? How do we get to the "affordable" in the Affordable Care Act? The United States is presently borrowing over 40 cents of every federal dollar it spends, and will approximately double the number of people over 65 in the next 30 years while, we hope, adding the 48 million presently uncovered by health insurance.

How do we afford this burden? The United States already spends 50 percent more than any other developed country on healthcare, and now we will be adding tens of millions of additional people to our inefficient system. The ACA contains a number of promising pilot programs in the area of cost containment, but we can suggest nothing equal to the magnitude of the problem.

The law creates a new institution, the Patient-Centered Outcomes Research Institute, which is to examine "relative health outcomes, clinical effectiveness, and appropriateness" of different medical treatments. A 19-member board that includes the stakeholders of the healthcare system governs the institute. If this new body is given some new powers, so it can truly engage in comparative effectiveness research, it may be an important tool in controlling costs. But the mega-question remaining is whether Americans have the maturity to accept that no healthcare system can do everything for everybody and must ultimately set limits.

We remain optimistic that in the judgment of history, the Affordable Care Act will prove to be the breakthrough America needs to expand its coverage, control its costs, and allow it to join the rest of the developed world in having a comprehensive and affordable healthcare system.

## Closing Remarks by Dr. Sharma

WE HOPE OUR READERS LEARNED ABOUT PAST AND CURRENT TRENDS IN HEALTHCARE and are more knowledgeable about the research surrounding the aging population, diabetes, obesity, and technology. Given the passage of certain parts of the Patient Protection and Affordable Care Act (ACA) and President Obama's reelection, we would like to conclude by briefly examining the future of healthcare costs. According to the Office of the Actuary at the Centers for Medicare and Medicaid Services (CMS), healthcare spending is projected to grow nearly 6 percent per year from 2010 to 2020. The CMS economists suggest, "the projected growth rate in healthcare spending is only slightly faster than spending would have been projected to grow in the absence of the Affordable Care Act" (Fleming, 2011). Although some may disagree with this assessment, and the actual outcome remains to be seen, many experts agree that healthcare spending will continue to increase and will account for nearly 20 percent of GDP by 2020. In addition, the share of government spending in healthcare will increase by an additional 4 percent from 2010 to 2020.

What can be done to contain some of these costs? We have presented a strong case for education, the importance of preventive services, the advantages of certain technological developments, and limits to high-end and unnecessary healthcare as potential solutions, but we can and should do more. A current article by Donald M. Berwick and Andrew D. Hackbarth in the *Journal of the American Medical Association* highlights the importance of eliminating waste in the healthcare industry. They draw attention to waste resulting from failures of care delivery, care coordination, overtreatment, administrative complexity, pricing failures, fraud, and abuse. Reorganizing healthcare to reduce, or even eliminate, such failures could have significant savings. However, this also warrants major changes in corporate and hospital cultures as well as a recognition that business strategies should also value relationships. Change is not easy, but President Obama and his administration have made strides, and perhaps continued improvements will have a positive long-term impact.

Although we are unable to offer a complete assessment of healthcare costs at this point, due to some recent and ongoing developments, we remain optimistic that a small part of the costs can be contained, but this requires everyone do their part. Therefore, we would like to conclude by focusing on you, the reader. Taking proactive measures to learn more about healthcare is a good decision and a wise investment. We encourage you to seek other reading material, visit online sources (some are listed below), and engage in a dialogue with your friends, family, and colleagues.

**Interested readers may want to visit the following websites:**

www.health.gov

www.healthcare.gov

www.healthfinder.gov

www.health.nih.gov

www.cdc.gov (Centers for Disease Control)

www.womenshealth.gov

www.medicare.gov

www.girlshealth.gov

www.who.int (World Health Organization)

www.aarp.org/health/ (AARP)

www.aoa.gov/AoARoot/Elders_Families

www.americanheart.org

**References**

Berwick, D. M., & Hackbarth, A. D. (2012). Eliminating waste in US health care. *JAMA: the journal of the American Medical Association, 307*(14), 1513-1516.

Fleming, Chris. (July 28, 2011).

Retrieved from http://healthaffairs.org/blog/2011/07/28/u-s-health-spend ing-projected-to-grow-5-8-percent-annually/

# Notes

### One: Aging

1. Christine K. Cassel, Mark A. Rudberg, and Jay Olshanksy, "The Price of Success: Health Care in an Aging Society," *Health Affairs* 11, no. 2 (1992).

2. Allan Pifer and Lydia Bronte, eds*., Our Aging Society: Paradox and Promise* (New York: W. W. Norton, 1986).

3. Jacob Siegel and Cynthia Tauber, "Demographic Dimensions of an Aging Population," in *Our Aging Society: Paradox and Promise*, eds. Allan Pifer and Lydia Bronte (New York: W. W. Norton, 1986).

4. James Lubitz, et al., "Three Decades of Health Care Use by the Elderly 1965–1998," *Health Affairs* 20, no. 2 (2001).

5. J. M. Guralnik, "The Compression of Morbidity: The Challenge Posed by Increasing Disability in the Years Prior to Death," *Journal of Aging and Health* (1991).

6. R. A. Reeves and E. Chen, "Who Wants to Eliminate Heart Disease?" *Journal of Clinical Epidemiology* 47, no. 6 (1991): 667–70.

7. There are various explanations as to why females have a longer life span, and a fairly systematic review is undertaken by Jen'nan Ghazal Read and Bridget Gorman in the *Annual Review of Sociology, 2010*. One can delineate the factors into the following considerations: behavioral, biological, social-structural, and psychosocial. There exists a large body of literature suggesting men are more likely to engage in risky and harmful behavior such as heavy drinking and smoking. Men are also more probable to experiment with illegal drugs, forgo wearing a seat belt, and skip preventive healthcare visits. These behavioral differences result in higher mortality at younger ages for men.

8. Jeff Williamson and Marco Pahor "Evidence Regarding the Benefits of Physical Exercise," *Archives of Internal Medicine* 170, no. 2 (2010).

9. However, one should be careful to note that these are mean effects and health returns to education can vary.

**Two: "The Problem": Thinking about the US Healthcare System**

1. Howard Brody and Franklin Miller, "The Internal Morality of Medicine," *Journal of Law, Medicine, and Ethics.*
2. Robert Blank, *The Price of Life: The Future of American Health Care* (New York: Columbia University Press, 1997).
3. J. B. McKinlay and S. M. McKinlay, "The Questionable Contribution of Medical Measures to the Decline of Mortality in the United States in the Twentieth Century," *The Milbank Memorial Fund Quarterly* 55, no. 3 (1977): 405-428.
4. Laurene Graig, *Health of Nations: An International Perspective on US Health Care Reform* (Washington, DC: CQ Press, 1991).
5. Victor Fuchs, "What Every Philosopher Should Know About Health Economics," *Journal of Health Economics* (June 1996).
6. J. Figueras and R. Saltman, "Analyzing the Evidence on European Health Care Reforms," *Health Affairs* 17, no. 2 (1998).
7. E. O. Attinger, *High Technology: The Pendulum Must Swing Back* (World Health Forum, 1987).
8. Eileen Crimmins, *Trends in Health Among the American Population* (Westport, CT: Praeger, 1993).
9. H. Aaron and C. Schultz, *Setting Domestic Priorities: What Can Government Do?* (Washington, DC: The Brookings Institute, 1992).
10. Sam Cordes, "The Economics of Health Services" (University Park: Pennsylvania State University, Cooperative Extension Service, 1982).
11. Alan Wertheimer, "Statistical Lives," *The New York Times*, April 25, 1980.
12. Mark L. Berk and Alan C. Monheit, "The Concentration of Health Care Expenditures, Revisited," *Health Affairs* 20, no. 2 (2001).

**Three: Rebuilding the House of Healthcare**

1. Elinor Ostrom, "A Behavioral Approach to the Rational Choice Theory of Collective Action," *American Political Science Review* 92, no. 1 (1998): 1-22.
2. Ibid.
3. Ibid.

4.  Paul Starr, *The Social Transofrmation of Medicine* (New York: Basic Books, 1982).

5.  L. Etheridge and S. Jones, "Managing a Pluralist Health System," *Health Affairs* 10, no. 4 (1991): 93-105.

6.  L. A. Katz, "How Far Will Population-Based Medicine Take Us?" *HMO Practice* 11, no. 3 (1997): 102-3.

7.  Guido Calabresi and Philip Bobbitt, *Tragic Choices* (New York: Norton, 1978).

8.  Christopher Robbin, "The Ethical Challenge of Rationing," in *The End of an Illusion: The Future of Health Policy in Western Industrialized Nations*, eds. Jean de Kervasdoue, John Kimberly, and Victor Rodwin (Berkeley: Univ. of California Press, 1984).

9.  V. R. Fuchs, "Ethics and Economies. Antagonists or Allies in Making Health Policy?" *Western Journal of Medicine* 168, no. 3(1998): 213-6.

10. Norman Daniels, "Health Care Needs and Distributive Justice," *Philosophy and Public Affairs* 10, no. 2 (1981): 146-179, emphasis added.

11. Haavi Morreim, "Medicine Meets Resource Limits: Restructuring the Legal Standards of Care," *University of Pittsburgh Law Review* 59, no. 1 (1997): 1-22.

12. David Eddy, "The Individual vs. Society: Is There a Conflict?" *The Journal of the American Medical Association* 265, no. 11 (1991).

13. Y. Claire Wang, Klim McPherson, Tim Marsh, Steven L Gortmaker, and Martin Brown, "Health and economic burden of the projected obesity trends in the USA and the UK," *The Lancet* 378, no. 3 (2011): 815-25.

14. A recent study by Wang et al. (2011) suggests "extrapolation of the historic trend in the USA would project an increase in annual medical cost from treating obesity-related disorders of US $28 (95% CI 8–49) billion per year by 2020 and $66 (95% CI 19–112) billion per year by 2030" (page 818). These scholars highlight the top contributors as arthritis, coronary heart disease, and diabetes.

15. Tape provided courtesy of *The Denver Post*.

16. During the past five years, this increase approximated less than 6 percent annually.

17. Revascularization is a much safer procedure for those without diabetes and under age 75.

**Four: Rethinking the Institutions of an Aging Society**

1. Robert Veatch, *Case Studies in Medical Ethics* (Cambridge: Harvard Univ. Press, 1979).
2. Frank Lewins, *Bioethics for Health Professionals* (Palgrave Macmillan, 1997).

# Selected Bibliography

Braveman, P. A., S. Egerter, C. Cubbin, D. R. Williams, and E. Pamuk. "Socioeconomic Disparities in Health in the United States: What the Patterns Tell Us." *American Journal of Public Health* 100, Suppl. 1 (2010): S186–S196.

Callahan, Daniel. *Taming the Beloved Beast: How Medical Technology Costs Are Destroying Our Health Care System*. Princeton, NJ: Princeton Univ. Press, 2009.

Colditz, G. A. "Economic costs of obesity." *The American Journal of Clinical Nutrition* 55, no. 2 (1992).

Conti, G., and J. J. Heckman. "Understanding the Early Origins of the Education-Health Gradient: A Framework That Can Also Be Applied to Analyze Gene-Environment Interactions." *Perspectives on Psychological Science* 5, no. 5 (2010): 585–605.

Cutler, D. M., and A. Lleras-Muney. "Understanding Differences in Health Behaviors by Education." *Journal of Health Economics* 29, no. 1 (2010): 1–28.

Deaton, Angus. "Policy Implications of the Gradient of Health and Wealth." *Health Affairs* 21, no. 2 (2002): 13.

Erickson, W., C. Lee, and S. von Schrader. *2008 Disability Status Report: The United States*. Ithaca, NY: Cornell Univ. Rehabilitation Research and Training Center on Disability Demographics and Statistics, 2010.

Finkelstein, E. A., M. D. DiBonaventura, S. M. Burgess, and B. C. Hale. "The Costs of Obesity in the Workplace." *Journal of Occupational and Environmental Medicine* 52, no. 10 (2010): 971–976.

Gordon, Colin. *Dead on Arrival: The Politics of Health Care in Twentieth-Century America*. Princeton, NJ: Princeton Univ. Press, 2003.

Hanson, C. William. *The Edge of Medicine: The Technology That Will Change Our Lives.* New York: Palgrave Macmillan, 2008.

Ogden, Cynthia L. *Obesity and Socioeconomic Status in Adults: United States, 2005–2008.* Hyattsville, MD: US Department of Health and Human Services, Centers for Disease Control and Prevention, National Center for Health Statistics, 2010.

Okie, Susan. "Home Delivery—Bringing Primary Care to the Housebound Elderly." *New England Journal of Medicine* 359, no. 23 (2008): 2409–2412.

Quadagno, Jill S. *One Nation, Uninsured: Why the US Has No National Health Insurance.* New York: Oxford Univ. Press, 2005.

Read, Jen'nan Ghazal, and Bridget K. Gorman. "Gender and Health Inequality." *Annual Review of Sociology* 36, no. 1 (2010): 371–386.

Riley, James C. *Poverty and Life Expectancy: The Jamaica Paradox.* Cambridge, UK: Cambridge Univ. Press, 2005.

———. *Rising Life Expectancy: A Global History.* Cambridge, UK: Cambridge Univ. Press, 2001.

Schimpff, Stephen C. *The Future of Medicine: Megatrends in Health Care That Will Improve Your Quality of Life.* Nashville: Thomas Nelson, 2007.

Sepulveda M. J., F. Tait, E. Zimmerman, and D. Edington. "Impact of Childhood Obesity on Employers." *Health Affairs* 29, no. 3 (2010): 513–521.

Skocpol, Theda. *Boomerang: Clinton's Health Security Effort and the Turn against Government in US Politics.* New York: W. W. Norton, 1996.

Trasande, L., D. Savitz, M. Lee, Y. Liu, and M. Weitzman. "Incremental Charges, Costs, and Length of Stay Associated with Obesity As a Secondary Diagnosis among Pregnant Women." *Medical Care* 47, no. 10 (2009): 1046–1052.

Wang, Y. C., K. McPherson, T. Marsh, S. L. Gortmaker, and M. Brown. "Health and economic burden of the projected obesity trends in the USA and the UK." *The Lancet* 378, no. 9793 (2011): 815–825.

Williamson J., and M. Pahor. "Evidence Regarding the Benefits of Physical Exercise." *Archives of Internal Medicine* 170, no. 2 (2010): 124–125.

# Permissions

### One: Aging

"The Crime of the Century," *Christian Science Monitor*, July 8, 1996.

"Good Neighbors, Bad Ancestors," *The Harvard Crimson*, December 4, 1997. All rights reserved. Reprinted by permission © The Harvard Crimson, Inc.

### Two: "The Problem": Thinking about the US Healthcare System

"Living on the Banks of Denial," Michigan Health & Hospitals (September/October 2001). Reprinted by permission.

"What If It Were Your Mother?," *Healthplan* (July/August 2001). Reprinted from *Healthplan* magazine by permission of the American Association of Health Plans.

"Doctors Have Patients, Governors Have Citizens," *Health Affairs* (September/October 2000).

"Better Healthcare through Rationing," *Allocating Healthcare Resources*, eds. James M. Humber and Robert F. Almeder (Totowa, NJ: Humana Press, 1995).

"Death: Right or Duty?" *Cambridge Quarterly of Healthcare Ethics* 6 (Winter 1997). Reprinted by permission of the Cambridge University Press.

### Three: Rebuilding the House of Healthcare

"The Case against Making Healthcare a Right," *Human Rights* 25, no. 4 (Fall 1998). Reprinted by permission.

"Redrawing the Ethics Map," *Hastings Center Report* (March/April 1999). Reprinted by permission © The Hastings Center.

# About the Authors

Richard D. Lamm is codirector of the Institute for Public Policy Studies at the University of Denver and a former three-term governor of Colorado (1975–1987). He is both a lawyer and a certified public accountant. He joined the faculty of the University of Denver in 1969 and has, except for his years as governor, been associated with the university ever since.

Lamm was chairman of the Pew Health Professions Commission and a public member of the Accreditation Council for Graduate Medical Education. He is the author of numerous articles on healthcare that have appeared in such medical publications as *The Journal of the American Medical Association*, *Health Affairs*, and *The Journal of Medical Economics*. He is a consultant to the National Conference of State Legislatures' Health Priorities Project and cochair of the Healthcare Priorities Planning Group through the National Conference of State Legislatures, The Hastings Center, and the Center for Public Policy and Contemporary Issues at the University of Denver.

Lamm has appeared on virtually every national news program, including *Buchanan & Press*, *Larry King Live*, *Inside*

*Politics, Today, Meet the Press, Good Morning America, Lehrer NewsHour,* and *Face the Nation.* His editorials have appeared in the *San Francisco Chronicle, The New York Times, The Christian Science Monitor, Newsday, The Boston Globe, Los Angeles Times,* and *Chicago Tribune.*

Wayne Armstrong/University of Denver

Andy Sharma is a political economist whose areas of specialty include aging, health disparities, later-life migration, and quantitative methods. He is the senior economist at the Institute for Public Policy Studies at the University of Denver, where he teaches graduate courses in cost-benefit analysis, microeconomics and policy, and quantitative methods. Sharma completed his doctorate in policy analysis with a minor in sociology from the University of North Carolina at Chapel Hill, where he was awarded grants from the National Institute on Aging and the National Institute of Child Health and Human Development (through Carolina Population Center). While at UNC, Sharma was also presented the Weiss Urban Livability Fellowship and the IMPACT Award. He holds a master's in mathematics from Loyola University and a master's in economics from DePaul University.